First World War
and Army of Occupation
War Diary
France, Belgium and Germany

48 DIVISION
Divisional Troops
243 South Midland Brigade Royal Field Artillery
31 March 1915 - 18 October 1916

WO95/2750/2

The Naval & Military Press Ltd
www.nmarchive.com
Published in association with The National Archives

Published by

The Naval & Military Press Ltd

Unit 10 Ridgewood Industrial Park,

Uckfield, East Sussex,

TN22 5QE England

Tel: +44 (0) 1825 749494

www.naval-military-press.com

www.nmarchive.com

This diary has been reprinted in facsimile from the original. Any imperfections are inevitably reproduced and the quality may fall short of modern type and cartographic standards.

© **Crown Copyright**
Images reproduced by permission of The National Archives, London, England, 2015.

Contents

Document type	Place/Title	Date From	Date To
Heading	WO95/2750/2		
Heading	48th Division 4th Sth Mid'd Bde RFA Became:- 243rd Bde RFA (Sth Mid'd) Apr 1915-Oct 1916		
Heading	1/4 S. Midland (Hrs) Bde RFA Vol I 31.3-30.4.15 Oct 16		
War Diary	Havre	31/03/1915	01/04/1915
War Diary	Steenwerck	02/04/1915	02/04/1915
War Diary	Menegatte	03/04/1915	04/04/1915
War Diary	Petit Pont	05/04/1915	17/04/1915
War Diary	La Menegatte	18/04/1915	30/04/1915
Heading	48th Division 1/4th S.M. Bde RFA Vol II 1-31.5.15		
War Diary	La Menegatte	01/05/1915	13/05/1915
War Diary	Ploegsteert	14/05/1915	31/05/1915
Heading	48th Division 4th S.M. Bde R.F.A. Vol III 1-20.6.15		
Heading	War Diary Of The 4th South Midland Field Artillery Brigade (How) From June 1st 1915 To June 30th 1915 (Volume III)		
War Diary	Ploegsteert	01/06/1915	26/06/1915
War Diary	Bailleul	27/06/1915	27/06/1915
War Diary	Vieux Berquin	28/06/1915	28/06/1915
War Diary	Robecq	29/06/1915	29/06/1915
War Diary	Ferfay	30/06/1915	30/06/1915
Heading	48th Division 1/4th S.M Bde R.F.A. Vol IV 1-31.7.15		
Heading	War Diary Of 1/4th Sth Mid Field Artillery Bde (How) T.F. From July 1st 1915 To July 31st 1915 (Volume 12)		
War Diary	Ferfay	01/07/1915	19/07/1915
War Diary	Thievres	20/07/1915	21/07/1915
War Diary	Authie	22/07/1915	26/07/1915
War Diary	Hebuterne	27/07/1915	31/07/1915
Heading	48th Division 1/4 S.M. Field Arty Bde Vol V From 1-31.8.15		
Heading	War Diary Of The 1/4th Sth Mid. Field Artillery Bde (How) T.F. From August 1st 1915 To August 31st 1915 (Volume 13)		
War Diary	Hebuterne	01/08/1915	31/08/1915
Heading	48th Division 1/4th S.M. Bde R.F.A. Vol VI Sept 1.15		
Heading	War Diary Of The 1/4th Sth Mid. Field Artillery Bde (How) T.F. From September 1st 1915 To September 30th 1915 (Volume 14)		
War Diary	Hebuterne	01/09/1915	30/09/1915
Heading	48th Division 4th S.M. Bde R.F.A. Vol VII Oct 15		
Heading	War Diary Of 1/4th Sth. Mid. Field. Artillery Brigade. (How) From October 1st 1915 To October 31st 1915 (Volume 15)		
War Diary	Hebuterne	01/10/1915	31/10/1915
Heading	48th Division 1/4th S.M. Bde. R.F.A. Nov 1915 Vol VIII		
War Diary	Hebuterne	01/11/1915	30/11/1915
Heading	1/4th Sth. Mid. Bde. R.F.A. (How) Dec Vol IX		

Heading	War Diary Of 1/4th Sth Mid. Field Artillery Brigade (Howitzer) From 1st December 1915 To 31st December 1915 (Volume 17)		
War Diary	Hebuterne	01/12/1915	31/12/1915
Heading	1/4 S M Bde R.F.A. Jan Vol X		
War Diary	Hebuterne	01/01/1916	31/01/1916
Heading	Appendix I To War Diary (Volume 18) Of 1/4th Sth. Mid. Field Artillery Brigade Howitzer		
War Diary		06/04/1915	11/04/1915
War Diary	Le Bizet	22/04/1915	20/06/1915
Heading	War Diary Of 1/4th Sth. Mid. Field Artillery Brigade (Howitzer) From 1st February 1916 To 29th February 1916 (Volume XI)		
War Diary	Hebuterne	01/02/1916	29/02/1916
Heading	War Diary Of 1/4th Sth. Mid. Field Artillery Brigade (Howitzer) From 1st March 1916 To 31st March 1916 (Volume XIII)		
War Diary	Hebuterne	01/03/1916	31/03/1916
Heading	War Diary Of 1/4th Sth. Mid. Field Artillery Brigade (Howitzer) From 1st April 1916 To 30th April 1916 (Volume 21)		
War Diary	Hebuterne	01/04/1916	30/04/1916
Heading	War Diary Of 243rd Brigade R.F.A. (Late 1/4th Sth Mid Field Artillery Brigade Howitzer) From 1st May 1916 To 31st May 1916 (Volume 22)		
War Diary	Hebuterne	01/05/1916	10/05/1916
War Diary	St. Leger	11/05/1916	31/05/1916
Heading	War Diary Of 243rd Brigade R.F.A. From 1st June 1916 To 30th June 1916 (Volume 23)		
War Diary	St. Leger	01/06/1916	03/06/1916
War Diary	Sailly-Au-Bois	04/06/1916	13/06/1916
War Diary	St. Leger	14/06/1916	30/06/1916
Heading	War Diary Of 243rd Brigade R.F.A. From 1st July 1916 To 31st July 1916 (Volume 24)		
War Diary	Mailly Maillet	01/07/1916	02/07/1916
War Diary	St. Leger	03/07/1916	05/07/1916
War Diary	Colincamps	06/07/1916	09/07/1916
War Diary	Courcelles	10/07/1916	20/07/1916
War Diary	St. Leger	21/07/1916	21/07/1916
War Diary	Aveluy	22/07/1916	27/07/1916
War Diary	Bouzincourt	28/07/1916	28/07/1916
War Diary	Ampliers	29/07/1916	29/07/1916
War Diary	St. Ouen	30/07/1916	31/07/1916
Heading	48th Divisional Artillery 243rd (South Midland) Brigade Royal Field Artillery August 1916		
Heading	War Diary Of 243rd Brigade R.F.A. From 1st August 1916 To 31st August 1916 (Volume 18)		
War Diary	St Ouen	01/08/1916	08/08/1916
War Diary	Amplier	09/08/1916	11/08/1916
War Diary	Bouzincourt	12/08/1916	12/08/1916
War Diary	Ovillers	13/08/1916	27/08/1916
War Diary	Bouzincourt	28/08/1916	31/08/1916
Heading	48th Divisional Artillery 243rd Brigade R.F.A. September 1916		
Heading	War Diary Of 243rd (S.M) Bde R.F.A. From 1st September 1916 To 30th September 1916 (Volume 19)		

War Diary	Bouzincourt	01/09/1916	15/09/1916
War Diary	Ovillers	16/09/1916	30/09/1916
Heading	War Diary Of 243rd (S.M) Brigade R.F.A. From 1st October To 18th October 1916 (Volume 27)		
War Diary	Ovillers	01/10/1916	01/10/1916
War Diary	Warlincourt	02/10/1916	18/10/1916
Miscellaneous	The Writer Has Not Been Informed Of The Action Taken By This Office		
Miscellaneous	Set A		

WO 05/27501 2/05/12

48TH DIVISION

4TH STH MID'D BDE RFA.
BECAME:-
243RD BDE RFA (STH MID'D)
APR 1915-OCT 1916.

BDE BROKEN UP

131/5195

1/4 S. Midland (Hvs) Bde RFA.

Vol 1 31.3 — 30.4.15

243 "Sh note   Oct 16

Army Form C. 2118.

WAR DIARY
or
INTELLIGENCE SUMMARY.
(Erase heading not required.)

Instructions regarding War Diaries and Intelligence Summaries are contained in F.S. Regs., Part II. and the Staff Manual respectively. Title pages will be prepared in manuscript.

Hour, Date, Place	Summary of Events and Information	Remarks and references to Appendices
Havre 31/3/15	Brigade arrived Havre about 8 a.m. Disembarked and proceeded to No. 2 Rest Camp for the night.	SHK

Army Form C. 2118.

WAR DIARY
or
INTELLIGENCE SUMMARY.
(Erase heading not required.)

Instructions regarding War Diaries and Intelligence Summaries are contained in F.S. Regs., Part II. and the Staff Manual respectively. Title pages will be prepared in manuscript.

Hour, Date, Place	Summary of Events and Information	Remarks and references to Appendices
1/4/15. Havre	Left Rest Camp and proceeded to the Gare de Maritime Havre, and entrained for Railhead. 3 days supplies for men and horses were put on the train and Iron Rations issued to men. The Train Wagons were also filled with 1 days supplies for men and horses. Left Havre at 10.30 a.m.	8K
2/4/15 Steenwerck	Arrived Steenwerck (Railhead) at 8 am detrained and went into billets at Merregatte. Attached to 4th Division with orders to take over positions from the 4th North Midland Howitzer Brigade. Colonel and Adjutant proceeded to Petit-Pont (the Headquarters of the North Midland Howitzer 34th Battery Commanders and arranged details for taking over.	8K
3/4/15 Merregatte	Proceeded to their observing stations and were shown their respective zones.	8K
4/4/15 Merregatte	Battery Commanders again proceeded to observing stations. Orders received to occupy Gun Position as follows:—	

(9 29 6) W 2794 100,000 8/14 H W V Forms/C. 2118/11.

WAR DIARY or INTELLIGENCE SUMMARY.

(Erase heading not required.)

Army Form C. 2118.

Instructions regarding War Diaries and Intelligence Summaries are contained in F.S. Regs., Part II. and the Staff Manual respectively. Title pages will be prepared in manuscript.

Hour, Date, Place	Summary of Events and Information	Remarks and references to Appendices
4/4/15 Continued	5th Battery to take over from 1st Battery Nth. Mid. Howitzers on the night 5th – 6th April. Hd. Qrs. Staff and 4th Battery to take over from 2nd Battery Nth. Mid. Howitzers on the night 6th – 7th April. 4th Battery to detach one section and send to Le Bizet. They are to be under the orders of O.C. 27th Brigade.	SN
5/4/15 Petit Pont.	5th Warwick Battery took over gun positions from 1st Derby Battery and moved in at 9 p.m.	SN
6/4/15 "	Headquarters Staff took over from Nth. Mid. Howitzers at 2 p.m. and 4th Battery took over gun positions from 2nd Derby Battery, one section being detached and attached to 14th R.F. Field Arty. Bde. at La Bizet. 10th Infantry Bde. rang up Hd Qrs. and asked for a Battery to shell Petit Douve Farm. Fired 6 rounds. It judged effective.	SN
7/4/15 "	The Spy House (an Observing Station of 5th Battery) was shelled at 10·0 a.m. 15 rounds were fired. 5 did not explode.	SN

WAR DIARY
or
INTELLIGENCE SUMMARY.

(Erase heading not required.)

Army Form C. 2118.

Hour, Date, Place	Summary of Events and Information	Remarks and references to Appendices
7/4/15 Continued.	No damage resulted. At mid-day slain observing station of 5th Battery at La Hutte Chateaux was heavily shelled and destroyed. No casualties. 4th Battery registered their night lines.	8K
8/4/15 Petit Pont.	5th Battery registered trenches at Cross Roads S.S.W. of Messines. 4th Battery registered night lines on "The Factory".	8K
9/4/15 Petit Pont.	5th Battery registered the Iroune Farm and communication trenches near Cross Roads S. of Messines. A detached section of the 4th Battery engaged near La Bizet fired 40 rounds. Commenced repairing observing station at La Hutte Chateaux. Great activity displayed by enemy near La Petite Douve Farm. Continuous gun and rifle fire all night. 5th Battery fired 2 rounds at German Communication trenches behind La Petite Douve Farm at midnight. Bombardier Hickman Killed.	8K

Army Form C. 2118.

WAR DIARY
or
INTELLIGENCE SUMMARY.
(Erase heading not required.)

Instructions regarding War Diaries and Intelligence Summaries are contained in F.S. Regs., Part II. and the Staff Manual respectively. Title pages will be prepared in manuscript.

Hour, Date, Place	Summary of Events and Information	Remarks and references to Appendices
10/4/15 Petit Pont.	5th Battery registered on house supposed to contain German machine work.	RK
11/4/15 Petit Pont.	Church Parade at 9.30 a.m. at Headquarters. Germans shelled 135th Battery horse-lines. 5th Battery fired 4 rounds at Messines after dark as the rumbling of a German convoy could be heard. The Spy Hole was again shelled, also the Chateau.	RK
12/4/15 Petit Pont.	Germans again shelled 135th Battery horse-lines but did no damage. 4th Battery fired 8 rounds registering targets. Germans shelled garden wall of Chateau. At 4.45 pm Irish Fusiliers were very heavily shelled by German heavy guns and called urgently for help. 5th Battery fired 26 rounds at the Petit Douve trenches and received following message from O.C. Irish Fusiliers. "Our best thanks for your efficient help." 1 Gun — 5th Battery hit by German shells. Gun not badly damaged.	RK

WAR DIARY
or
INTELLIGENCE SUMMARY.
(Erase heading not required.)

Army Form C. 2118.

Instructions regarding War Diaries and Intelligence Summaries are contained in F.S. Regs., Part II. and the Staff Manual respectively. Title pages will be prepared in manuscript.

Hour, Date, Place	Summary of Events and Information	Remarks and references to Appendices
12/4/15	Continued and no casualties to gun detachment. A very quiet night. No hostile gun fire at all.	
13/4/15 Petit Pont	A very quiet day. Nothing doing	SNK
14/4/15 Petit Pont	4th Battery fired at a house containing German snipers near La Gheer. Shell effective.	SNK
15/4/15 Petit Pont	5th Battery registered La Potene Farm and the "Rose House". Both of these targets were hit. 4th Battery fired at house containing snipers near La Gheer and put 7 shells into it.	SNK
16/4/15 Petit Pont	To quiet day. Nothing to report.	SNK
17/4/15 Petit Pont	Orders received for one section of 4th Battery and its Headquarters to proceed to a new position near Hoogeline.	SNK
18/4/15 La Menegatte	Headquarters handed over their billets and telephone lines to Hd. Qrs. 3rd Sh. Mid. Brigade and proceeded to billets near Menegatte. One section of 4th Battery moved to new position under cover of darkness.	SNK

Army Form C. 2118.

WAR DIARY
or
INTELLIGENCE SUMMARY.
(Erase heading not required.)

Instructions regarding War Diaries and Intelligence Summaries are contained in F.S. Regs., Part II. and the Staff Manual respectively. Title pages will be prepared in manuscript.

Hour, Date, Place	Summary of Events and Information	Remarks and references to Appendices
19/4/15 La Menegatte	Lieut. Wyley temporarily attached to 4th Battery for duty. 4th Battery now under orders of 4th Division.	GW
20/4/15 La Menegatte	5th Battery received orders to place one section in new position about 300 yards S.E. of their old position so as to cover zone between St. Yves and La Gheer.	GW
21/4/15 La Menegatte	The section of 5th Battery which was ordered to take up position 300 yards S.E. of their old position has not been ordered to take up position in Ploegsteert Wood which used to be occupied by section of 4th Battery.	GW
22/4/15 La Menegatte	The 5th Battery registered night-lines for section in new position. 4th Battery registered targets near Frelinghien.	GW
23/4/15 La Menegatte	The 4th and 5th Batteries continued to register targets in their respective zones.	GW
24/4/15 & 25/4/15 La Menegatte	Nothing to report.	GW
26/4/15 La Menegatte	Lieut. Davidson, R.A.M.C. (T) temporarily attached to 4th Bty.	GW

(9 29 6) W 2794 100,000 8/14 H W V Forms/C. 2118/11.

Army Form C. 2118.

WAR DIARY
or
INTELLIGENCE SUMMARY.
(Erase heading not required.)

Instructions regarding War Diaries and Intelligence Summaries are contained in F.S. Regs., Part II. and the Staff Manual respectively. Title pages will be prepared in manuscript.

Hour, Date, Place	Summary of Events and Information	Remarks and references to Appendices
26/4/15 Continued	Orders received for 5th Battery not to shoot except to retaliate when asked to do so by the Infantry.	SVK
27/4/15 La Menegatte	4. Battery registered targets near Frelinghien	SVK
28/4/15 La Menegatte	Nothing to report.	SVK
29/4/15 La Menegatte	Nothing to report.	SVK
30/4/15 La Menegatte	Nothing to report.	SVK

121/502

8th Division.

1/4th Bn. S.M. Bde. R.F.A.

Vol III 1 — 31.5.15

WAR DIARY
or
INTELLIGENCE SUMMARY.

(*Erase heading not required.*)

Army Form C. 2118.

Instructions regarding War Diaries and Intelligence Summaries are contained in F. S. Regs., Part II. and the Staff Manual respectively. Title pages will be prepared in manuscript.

Hour, Date, Place	Summary of Events and Information	Remarks and references to Appendices
1.5.15 LA MENEGATTE	4th Battery registered targets near FRELINGHIEN. 5th Battery fired 18 rounds at LA PETITE DOUVE. Colonel and Adjutant visited firing trenches of 5th WARWICKS.	GJK
2.5.15 LA MENEGATTE	Lieut. Davidson rejoined from 4th Battery.	GJK
3.5.15 LA MENEGATTE	5th Battery registered communication trench just behind front line German trenches near MESSINES. Colonel and Adjutant went round trenches of 5th GLOUCESTERS.	GJK
4.5.15 LA MENEGATTE	5th Battery registered LA TRUIE FARM.	GJK
5.5.15 LA MENEGATTE	Colonel and Adjutant attended Conference of O.C. Brigades under General Butler, to discuss targets that have already been registered, and alternative positions for Batteries. 5th Battery fired 18 rounds at DRESDEN HOUSE.	GJK
6.5.15 LA MENEGATTE	Brigade issued with respirators.	GJK
7.5.15 LA MENEGATTE	20 Remounts received for the Brigade	GJK
8.5.15 LA MENEGATTE	Nothing to report.	GJK

Army Form C. 2118.

WAR DIARY
or
INTELLIGENCE SUMMARY.
(Erase heading not required.)

Instructions regarding War Diaries and Intelligence Summaries are contained in F.S. Regs., Part II. and the Staff Manual respectively. Title pages will be prepared in manuscript.

Hour, Date, Place	Summary of Events and Information	Remarks and references to Appendices
9.5.15 LA MENEGATTE	Demonstration along the whole front of the South Midland Division. 5th Battery fired at intervals during the day. At 7.0 pm fired 10 rounds into MESSINES.	GK
10.5.15 LA MENEGATTE	General Ross Johnson assumed Command of the R.A., 5th Mid. Divn.	GK
11.5.15 LA MENEGATTE	Nothing to report.	GK
12.5.15 LA MENEGATTE	5th Battery fired at the German trenches behind the BIRD CAGE and made very good practice.	GK
13.5.15 LA MENEGATTE	Received orders to move Headquarters nearer 5th Battery and to Command the two Sections of this Battery as a Brigade.	GK
14.5.15 PLOEGSTEERT	Headquarters Staff moved into new billets near PLOEGSTEERT WINDMILL.	GK
15.5.15 PLOEGSTEERT	Colonel and Adjutant inspected new gun positions for 5th Battery, if driven back to G.H.Q. line.	GK
16.5.15 PLOEGSTEERT	Nothing to report.	GK

Army Form C. 2118.

WAR DIARY
or
INTELLIGENCE SUMMARY.
(Erase heading not required.)

Instructions regarding War Diaries and Intelligence Summaries are contained in F. S. Regs., Part II. and the Staff Manual respectively. Title pages will be prepared in manuscript.

Place	Date	Hour	Summary of Events and Information	Remarks and references to Appendices
PLOEGSTEERT	17.5.15.	—	4th Battery changed their wagon line from PONT DE NIEPPE to farm near TROIS TILLEULS.	FK
PLOEGSTEERT	18.5.15.	—	Colonel and Adjutant reconnoitred alternative gun positions near PLOEGSTEERT WOOD. Two telephonists sent to G.H.Q for course of instruction in wireless telegraphy. Lieut. L.H. TAYLOR R.F.A., and 2nd Lieut. F.C. GEORGE R.F.A., from 23rd Division temporarily attached to 5th Battery for a fortnight.	FK
PLOEGSTEERT	19.5.15.	—	Adjutant organised visual signalling communications between observing stations and gun positions of 5th Battery.	FK
PLOEGSTEERT	20.5.15.	—	5th Battery registered two targets with aeroplane observation.	FK
PLOEGSTEERT	21.5.15.	—	5th Battery fired on German communication trenches near LE GHEER. New alternative gun position being made by 5th Battery.	FK
PLOEGSTEERT	22.5.15.	—	5th Battery shot at German communication trenches near LE GHEER.	FK
PLOEGSTEERT	23.5.15.	—	5th Battery fired at DRESDEN HOUSE.	FK
PLOEGSTEERT	24.5.15.	—	Adjutant attended conference re shooting in conjunction with aircraft. 5th Battery fired at a target near MESSINES, aeroplane observed fire and communicated to Battery by wireless.	FK
PLOEGSTEERT	25.5.15.	—	General Ford Johnson came to Headquarters and impressed on everybody the necessity of careful drill in adjusting respirators. 5th Battery registered targets, fire being observed by aeroplane.	FK

WAR DIARY or INTELLIGENCE SUMMARY.

Army Form C. 2118.

(Erase heading not required.)

Place	Date	Hour	Summary of Events and Information	Remarks and references to Appendices
PLOEGSTEERT	26.5.15	-	5th Battery fired in conjunction with aeroplanes.	PK
PLOEGSTEERT	27.5.15	-	5th Battery fired in conjunction with aeroplane. Germans shelled 5th Battery billets. Gunner Dunbar killed.	PK
PLOEGSTEERT	28.5.15	-	5th Battery fired at Snipers House in German front line trenches.	PK
PLOEGSTEERT	29.5.15	-	5th Battery fired at Snipers House and completely demolished it.	PK
PLOEGSTEERT	30.5.15	-	5th Battery fired in conjunction with aeroplane.	PK
PLOEGSTEERT	31.5.15	-	5th Battery fired at German front line trenches near LE GHEER.	PK

48th Division

6th I.M. Bde. R.F.A.

Vol III 1 — 30.6.15

181/584

CONFIDENTIAL.

WAR DIARY
of the

4th. South Midland Field Artillery Brigade (How).

From June 1st. 1915 to June 30th. 1915.

(Volume III).

---------oOo---------

CAPT., & ADJT.,
1/4th. S.M. FIELD ARTY., BDE., (HOW)

Army Form C. 2118.

WAR DIARY
or
INTELLIGENCE SUMMARY.
(Erase heading not required.)

Instructions regarding War Diaries and Intelligence Summaries are contained in F. S. Regs., Part II. and the Staff Manual respectively. Title pages will be prepared in manuscript.

Place	Date	Hour	Summary of Events and Information	Remarks and references to Appendices
PLOEGSTEERT	1.6.15	—	5th Battery fired at German anti-aircraft gun.	GK
PLOEGSTEERT	2.6.15	—	Nothing to report.	GK
PLOEGSTEERT	3.6.15	—	5th Battery fired at Snipers House near MESSINES and did good practice.	GK
PLOEGSTEERT	4.6.15	—	5th Battery fired at a house in the Birdcage and obtained two direct hits.	GK
PLOEGSTEERT	5.6.15	—	A.D.V.S. inspected the horses of the 5th Battery and Headquarters Staff. 5th Battery fired at Dresden House and did good practice. Colonel MULLINER came to see the Brigade.	GK
PLOEGSTEERT	6.6.15	—	Received secret orders about 1 am. that a mine was to be exploded in Birdcage and that 5th Battery was to co-operate. Mine exploded at 10.20 am. very successfully and 5th Battery did good practice on German trenches in the Birdcage. In the afternoon a German working party of twenty men was discovered repairing Birdcage. 5th Battery fired 1 round which dispersed the party, they did no more work that afternoon.	GK
PLOEGSTEERT	7.6.15	—	5th Battery fired at home containing machine guns opposite left of Warwick Infantry Brigade. Did good practice.	GK
PLOEGSTEERT	8.6.15	—	To conduct test signalling communication between forward visual station at LAGHEER and 5th Battery gun position.	GK
PLOEGSTEERT	9.6.15	—	5th Battery gun position fairly heavily shelled. No harm done. One shell burst in dug-out which had been evacuated when	GK

1577 Wt. W10791/1773 500,000 1/15 D. D. & L. A.D.S.S./Forms/C. 2118.

Army Form C. 2118.

WAR DIARY
or
INTELLIGENCE SUMMARY.
(Erase heading not required.)

Place	Date	Hour	Summary of Events and Information	Remarks and references to Appendices
PLOEGSTEERT	10.6.15		Battery was split up into two sections. 5th Battery fired at two houses used to contain snipers on MESSINES RIDGE. Both houses hit. The Germans exploded a mine near ST. YVES opposite T Trench. No damage done as mine exploded 5 yards short of trenches. Germans then opened heavy bombardment of PLOEGSTEERT WOOD and swept the PLOEGSTEERT - LA GHEER Road with rifle and machine gun fire. All artillery telephone wires were cut except our own. O.C. Brigade attended a gun demonstration at BAILLEUL.	OK
PLOEGSTEERT	11.6.15		5th Battery fired at LA POTTERIE Farm in conjunction with one of the Worcester Batteries. Effect good. The I.O.H. inspected the guns of the 5th Battery and they are to be overhauled one by one in the workshops. The guns themselves are undamaged, but the elevating gear of all guns require adjustment.	OK
PLOEGSTEERT	12.6.15		5th Battery fired at the Store House. Effect fair.	OK
PLOEGSTEERT	13.6.15		5th Battery fired on communication trenches at the back of LA PETITE DOUVE. Obtained direct hit on machine gun emplacement.	OK
PLOEGSTEERT	14.6.15		Germans exploded a mine near the Birdcage. Mine exploded short of our trenches and no damage resulted. They opened a heavy bombardment on PLOEGSTEERT WOOD immediately the mine was blown. Every telephone wire was cut except our own	OK

WAR DIARY
or
INTELLIGENCE SUMMARY.
(Erase heading not required.)

Army Form C. 2118.

Place	Date	Hour	Summary of Events and Information	Remarks and references to Appendices
PLOEGSTEERT	15.6.15	—	which worked perfectly all through. 5th Battery fired at horse supposed to be Headquarters of a Battalion situated on the MESSINES Ridge. Effect good. Burying all telephone wire liable to hostile shell fire.	OK
PLOEGSTEERT	16.6.15	—	5th Battery fired at BELHEEN in conjunction with 2nd Sh. Mid. F.A. Brigade, and also at PONT ROUGE.	OK
PLOEGSTEERT	17.6.15	—	Nothing to report.	OK
PLOEGSTEERT	18.6.15	—	A mine exploded near LA TOUQUET.	OK
PLOEGSTEERT	19.6.15	—	5th Battery fired at Long Barn and Swries Farm with the Right Section.	OK
PLOEGSTEERT	20.6.15	—	5th Battery fired at the Storehouse. One section 4th Battery came into action replacing Right section of 5th Battery, and Right section of 5th Battery came into action with the Left Section of 5th Battery. Second section of 4th Battery in billets near NIEPPE. All gun emplacements have been made for them.	OK
PLOEGSTEERT	21.6.15	—	4th Battery Headquarters billeted. Remainder of Battery bivouacing in PLOEGSTEERT WOOD. 4th Battery fired at the Bastion, and registered their night lines.	OK
PLOEGSTEERT	22.6.15	—	4th Battery registered their night lines.	OK
PLOEGSTEERT	23.6.15	—	4th Battery registered targets. 5th Battery fired at Lilleul and Communication Trench.	OK

Army Form C. 2118.

WAR DIARY
or
INTELLIGENCE SUMMARY.
(Erase heading not required.)

Instructions regarding War Diaries and Intelligence Summaries are contained in F. S. Regs., Part II. and the Staff Manual respectively. Title pages will be prepared in manuscript.

Place	Date	Hour	Summary of Events and Information	Remarks and references to Appendices
PLOEGSTEERT	24.6.15		Advance party of Canadian Howitzer Brigade arrived to take over. 5th Battery fired at Dresden House.	GW
PLOEGSTEERT	25.6.15		Nothing to report.	GW
PLOEGSTEERT	26.6.15		Canadian Howitzer Brigade took over from us in the evening, the two batteries moving out of their position at 9 p.m. Brigade then marched under cover of darkness to BAILLEUL, with Group "C" which consists of 144th Infantry Brigade; 1st Cdn. Mtd. Field Forty. Bde., 4th Howitzer Brigade, No 3 Coy. Train, No 3 Field Coy R.E. and 2nd Cdn. Mtd. Field Ambulance. Billeted in large farm.	GW
BAILLEUL	27.6.15		Marched with Group "C" to VIEUX BERQUIN and billeted in the town.	GW
VIEUX BERQUIN	28.6.15		Marched with Group "C" to ROBECQ via MERVILLE & CALONNE.	GW
ROBECQ	29.6.15		Marched with Group "C" to FERFAY via BUSNES and LILLERS. C.R.A. inspected the Brigade on the march and complimented them on the turn out and the condition of the horses. Billeted in the village.	GW
FERFAY	30.6.15		Brigade resting and probably will stop at FERFAY for a week.	GW

121/6272

48th Division

1/4th S.M. Bde R.F.A.

Vol IV

1-31 may 1915

Confidential.

War Diary
of
1/4th. Sth. Mid. Field Artillery Bde (How.) T.F.

From July 1st 1915 to July 31st 1915.

(Volume 12).

J S Kidd
CAPT., & ADJT.,
1/4th. S.M. FIELD ARTY., BDE., (HOW.)

Army Form C. 2118.

WAR DIARY
or
INTELLIGENCE SUMMARY.
(Erase heading not required.)

Instructions regarding War Diaries and Intelligence Summaries are contained in F. S. Regs., Part II. and the Staff Manual respectively. Title pages will be prepared in manuscript.

Place	Date	Hour	Summary of Events and Information	Remarks and references to Appendices
FERFAY	1.7.15	—	Nothing to report.	GK
FERFAY	2.7.15	9.0 am	4th & 5th Batteries paraded in drill order. Amm. Col. gunners, gun-drill.	GK
FERFAY	3.7.15	—	Batteries paraded in drill order.	GK
FERFAY	4.7.15	—	Kit Inspection. Batteries paraded in drill order.	GK
FERFAY	5.7.15	—	Battery drill order.	GK
FERFAY	6.7.15	—	Brigade and Battery staffs carried out night operations with 144th Infantry Brigade in the vicinity of BOIS DE MARQUET. Operations were continued with 144th Infy. Brigade until 6.0 am.	GK
FERFAY	7.7.15	—	Brigade Route March.	GK
FERFAY	8.7.15	—	Battery Drill Orders.	GK
FERFAY	9.7.15	—	Nothing to report.	GK
FERFAY	10.7.15	—	O.C. Brigade and O's. C. Batteries carried out reconnaissance in IV Corps area.	GK
FERFAY	11.7.15	—	Brigade Ordered to relieve 8th London Howitzer Brigade on the nights of 12-13th and 13-14th. One section from each Battery marched to MAZINGARBE. On arriving at their positions orders cancelling the relief were received.	GK
FERFAY	12.7.15	—		GK

WAR DIARY
or
INTELLIGENCE SUMMARY.

(Erase heading not required.)

Army Form C. 2118.

Place	Date	Hour	Summary of Events and Information	Remarks and references to Appendices
FERFAY	13.7.15	—	The section returned to FERFAY.	GMK
FERFAY	14.7.15	—	Nothing to report.	GMK
FERFAY	15.7.15	—	Brigade and Battery staffs paraded and practised taking up positions, near BAILLEUL LES PERNES.	GMK
FERFAY	16.7.15	—	Brigade and Battery staffs paraded in vicinity of FLORINGHEM.	GMK
FERFAY	17.7.15	—	Orders received that the Division would be transferred from IV Corps to VII Corps on 18th instant.	GMK
FERFAY	18.7.15	—	Nothing to report.	GMK
FERFAY	19.7.15	—	Lieut. Wyley and billeting party sent to DOULLENS by early morning train from LILLERS. In the afternoon H.Q. Battery and Brigade Hd. Qrs. staff left FERFAY and entrained at LILLERS at 5.40 p.m. for DOULLENS. On arrival at DOULLENS at 11 p.m. were sent on in same train to MONDICOURT, arriving there at midnight.	GMK
THIEVRES	20.7.15	—	Marched from MONDICOURT to THIEVRES and arrived there at 4 a.m. 5th Battery arriving there at 7 a.m. Village very small and troops had to bivouac.	GMK
THIEVRES	21.7.15	—	Ammunition Column arrived by train from LILLERS, and marched from MONDICOURT to AUTHIE. Remainder of Brigade moved to AUTHIE in the morning, then again had to bivouac. In the afternoon the O.C. VII Corps had a look round the Brigade.	GMK

WAR DIARY
or
INTELLIGENCE SUMMARY.
(Erase heading not required.)

Army Form C. 2118.

Place	Date	Hour	Summary of Events and Information	Remarks and references to Appendices
AUTHIE	22.7.15	—	Colonel and Battery Commanders went with the C.R.A. to SAILLY, where they met the French C.R.A. and arranged the occupying of gun positions.	JK
AUTHIE	23.7.15	—	Colonel and Battery Commanders went to HEBUTERNE, and reconnoitred gun positions.	JK
AUTHIE	24.7.15	—	The two Batteries started digging gun pits at HEBUTERNE. Colonel and Adjutant went round the different observing stations.	JK
AUTHIE	25.7.15	—	Started laying telephone wires from Brigade Hd. Qrs. in HEBUTERNE to Battery gun positions. Hd. Qr. Staff and 4th Battery billeted in village. 5th Battery in dug-outs.	JK
AUTHIE	26.7.15		Batteries digging gun positions. Capt. Saunders transferred to 2nd Amn. Col. as Adjutant. Capt. Field from 4th Battery to Command Ammunition Column. 2nd Lieut. Mottram posted to 4th Battery from Ammunition Column. Brigade moved by Batteries at 7.30 p.m. to HEBUTERNE. Two sections in action (one from each Battery).	JK
HEBUTERNE	27.7.15		Batteries laying telephone lines and generally settling into their new positions. 4th Battery digging gun pits for their remaining section.	JK

Army Form C. 2118.

WAR DIARY
or
INTELLIGENCE SUMMARY.

(Erase heading not required.)

Instructions regarding War Diaries and Intelligence Summaries are contained in F. S. Regs., Part II. and the Staff Manual respectively. Title pages will be prepared in manuscript.

Place	Date	Hour	Summary of Events and Information	Remarks and references to Appendices
HEBUTERNE	28.7.15	—	5th Battery has orders not to fire at present. 4th Battery registered night lines for two guns in the evening. In the afternoon one gun of 4th Battery came up from wagon line and occupied gun position. The fourth gun pit not ready so timber cannot be obtained at present.	F/K
HEBUTERNE	29.7.15	—	In the afternoon 4th Battery registered night line for gun that came into position the night before.	F/K
HEBUTERNE	30.7.15		4th Battery registered points in German trenches.	F/K
HEBUTERNE	31.7.15		Colonel and Adjutant made a reconnaissance of likely new observing stations, and alternative gun positions.	F/K

121/Hep

48th Division

1/4 S.M. Field Amby Rolls

Vol V

From 1- 31. 5. 15

Confidential

War Diary

of the

1/4th. Sth. Mid. Field Artillery Bde., (How) T.F.

From August 1st 1915, to August 31st 1915.

(Volume 13).

J H Kidd
CAPT., & ADJT.,
1/4th. S.M. FIELD ARTY., BDE., (HOW)

Army Form C. 2118.

WAR DIARY
or
INTELLIGENCE SUMMARY.
(Erase heading not required.)

Place	Date	Hour	Summary of Events and Information	Remarks and references to Appendices
HEBUTERNE	1.8.15	—	4th Battery registered farm SANS NOM and cross roads near it. Making two Brigade Observing Stations, one on the left and one on the right.	SK
HEBUTERNE	2.8.15	—	4th Battery fired at a working party and dispersed same.	SK
HEBUTERNE	3.8.15	—	Nothing to report.	SK
HEBUTERNE	4.8.15	—	Obtained leave to collect wood and bricks from HEBUTERNE. Batteries finishing their gun pits and observing stations, and starting to make brick standings in the horse lines.	SK
HEBUTERNE	5.8.15	—	4th Battery making a new observing station as their old one is being used by G.O.C. Division.	SK
HEBUTERNE	6.8.15	—	4th Battery fired at farm SANS NOM and had four direct hits. This Battery also registered left-hand corner of BOIS DU BIEZ. Arranged S.O.S. signals with 145th Infantry Brigade. Bricks can no longer be obtained for horse standings, all being required for Infantry trenches.	SK
HEBUTERNE	7.8.15	—	4th Battery fired at a German working party making a large trench near SERRE.	SK
HEBUTERNE	8.8.15	—	5th Battery fired at farm SANS NOM and made excellent practice. The farm is partly destroyed.	SK

Army Form C. 2118

WAR DIARY
or
INTELLIGENCE SUMMARY.
(Erase heading not required.)

Instructions regarding War Diaries and Intelligence Summaries are contained in F. S. Regs., Part II. and the Staff Manual respectively. Title pages will be prepared in manuscript.

Place	Date	Hour	Summary of Events and Information	Remarks and references to Appendices
HEBUTERNE	9.8.15	-	Very severe thunderstorm in the evening and trenches and dug-outs got very wet indeed.	S.M.
HEBUTERNE	10.8.15	-	Adjutant went to wagon lines and in conjunction with Staff Captain deleted new horse lines for the coming winter. Proper truss standings are to be laid down before the horses are put on to them.	S.M.
HEBUTERNE	11.8.15	-	5th Battery fired at a machine gun emplacement in conjunction with such Howitzers and French guns and made good shooting.	S.M.
HEBUTERNE	12.8.15	-	Nothing to report.	S.M.
HEBUTERNE	13.8.15	-	Brigade Major came and inspected gun pits of the Brigade and pointed out a new position for the two guns of the Brigade that are at present in reserve. 5th Battery fired at a trench mortar and knocked it out.	S.M.
HEBUTERNE	14.8.15	-	Germans have been sapping forward on our right for the last few days with the intention of making a new front line trench West of SERRE. At 4.30.a.m. the 4th Battery in conjunction with the Field Guns fired 14 rounds at this	S.M.

1577 Wt.W10791/1773 500,000 1/15 D. D. & L.   A.D.S.S./Forms/C. 2118.

WAR DIARY
or
INTELLIGENCE SUMMARY.

(Erase heading not required.)

Army Form C. 2118

Place	Date	Hour	Summary of Events and Information	Remarks and references to Appendices
	14-8-15	cont	sap. In the afternoon 4th Battery fired 10 more rounds at the sap and obtained 3 direct hits.	SMK
HEBUTERNE	15-8-15		4th Battery started digging new gun position for their left section. Capt. Lucas attached to 5th Battery for a week and Lieut. Wyley attached to D.A.C. for a week.	SMK
HEBUTERNE	16-8-15		4th Battery fired at a redoubt near SERRE.	SMK
HEBUTERNE	17-8-15		5th Battery registered a front line trench near farm SANS NOM and 4th Battery fired at redoubt near SERRE making effective practice.	SMK
HEBUTERNE	18-8-15		5th Battery fired on German front line trenches near farm SANS NOM. 4th Battery registered small house North of SERRE.	SMK
HEBUTERNE	19-8-15		5th Battery fired on front line trenches West of farm SANS NOM. 4th Battery registered trenches near SERRE.	SMK
HEBUTERNE	20-8-15		Germans shelled HEBUTERNE and in retaliation 5th Battery fired 4 rounds at GOMMECOURT. This Battery also fired 2 rounds at a German battery.	SMK

WAR DIARY
or
INTELLIGENCE SUMMARY.

(Erase heading not required.)

Army Form C. 2118.

Place	Date	Hour	Summary of Events and Information	Remarks and references to Appendices
HEBUTERNE	21-8-15		4th Battery fired at a house in SERRE supposed to be used as an observation station, obtaining 2 direct hits on the house.	GK
HEBUTERNE	22-8-15		5th Battery fired on German trenches and did some damage as stretcher bearers were seen to leave the trenches with wounded after this battery had ceased firing.	GK
HEBUTERNE	23-8-15		HEBUTERNE rather heavily shelled. 5th Battery in retaliation fired 6 rounds into GOMMECOURT.	GK
HEBUTERNE	24-8-15		5th Battery fired 2 rounds at German working party, dispersing same.	GK
HEBUTERNE	25-8-15		4th Battery fired at machine-gun emplacement West of SERRE.	GK
HEBUTERNE	26-8-15		Nothing to report.	GK
HEBUTERNE	27-8-15		5th Battery fired at a machine-gun emplacement.	GK
HEBUTERNE	28-8-15		Mr. Arthur Henderson and a deputation of Labour Members visited the Brigade and went round the gun positions, and then went into the trenches and saw 5th Battery fire 8 rounds at Farm SANS NOM. The shortage of ammunition was well rubbed into them.	GK

WAR DIARY
or
INTELLIGENCE SUMMARY.

(Erase heading not required.)

Army Form C. 2118.

Place	Date	Hour	Summary of Events and Information	Remarks and references to Appendices
HEBUTERNE	29.8.15	—	Lieut. Bassett of the 2/4th Sh. Mid. F.A. Brigade joined the Brigade and is attached to the 5th Battery.	S.K.
HEBUTERNE	30.8.15	—	4th Battery fired at German Front Line Trenches.	S.K.
HEBUTERNE	31.8.15	—	5th Battery fired at RETTENOYE Farm. Two guns of 4th Battery occupied new position just dug by them, and all eight guns of the Brigade are now in action.	S.K.

121/6918

48th Division

1/4th S.M. Bde R.F.A.

1st XC

Sep 1. 15.

Confidential.

WAR DIARY

of the

1/4th Sth. Mid. Field Artillery Bde. (How). T.F.

FROM September 1st 1915 TO September 30th 1915.

(Volume 14).

CAPT., & ADJT.,
1/4th. S.M. FIELD ARTY., BDE., (HOW)

Army Form C. 2118

WAR DIARY
or
INTELLIGENCE SUMMARY.
(Erase heading not required.)

Instructions regarding War Diaries and Intelligence Summaries are contained in F. S. Regs., Part II. and the Staff Manual respectively. Title pages will be prepared in manuscript.

Place	Date	Hour	Summary of Events and Information	Remarks and references to Appendices
HEBUTERNE	1-9-15	-	4th Battery registered LA LOUVIÈRE Farm from new gun position.	SK
HEBUTERNE	2-9-15	-	5th Battery registered a machine-gun emplacement. 4th Battery registered targets from new gun position.	SK
HEBUTERNE	3-9-15	-	5th Battery fired at German observation station. 4th Battery registered targets from new gun position.	SK
			Orders received to make two new gun pits to cover extension of our zone, 48th Division having taken over part of the line from 37th Division and now held FONQUEVILLERS; the 37th Division carrying on the line to the left from FONQUEVILLERS.	SK
HEBUTERNE	4-9-15	-	Nothing to report.	SK
HEBUTERNE	5-9-15	-	Section of 5th Battery whose zone includes GOMMECOURT Wood, now allowed to fire.	SK
HEBUTERNE	6-9-15	-	5th Battery registered GOMMECOURT Wood, and trenches near GOMMECOURT.	SK
HEBUTERNE	7-9-15	-	4th Battery fired on German trenches early in the morning, before German observation balloon was up. 5th Battery registered a German communication trench.	SK
HEBUTERNE	8-9-15	-	4th Battery registered targets with section in sunken road.	SK

Army Form C. 2118.

WAR DIARY
or
INTELLIGENCE SUMMARY.
(Erase heading not required.)

Instructions regarding War Diaries and Intelligence Summaries are contained in F. S. Regs., Part II. and the Staff Manual respectively. Title pages will be prepared in manuscript.

Place	Date	Hour	Summary of Events and Information	Remarks and references to Appendices
HEBUTERNE	8.9.15 (cont.)		5th Battery fired at machine-gun emplacement.	SJK
HEBUTERNE	9.9.15	—	5th Battery fired at a working party.	SJK
HEBUTERNE	10.9.15	—	Batteries doing during drill every morning at the wagon lines under the Adjutant.	SJK
HEBUTERNE	11.9.15		Germans shelled our trenches with a MINENWERFER and the 5th. Battery replied on GOMMECOURT WOOD and trenches. HEBUTERNE was shelled in the evening and we replied on GOMMECOURT.	SJK
HEBUTERNE	12.9.15		Selected new observing station so as to observe our fire on German trenches WEST of GOMMECOURT.	SJK
HEBUTERNE	13.9.15		Section of 4th. Battery in sunk road registered targets on the SERRE Front. 5th. Battery registered on trenches near GOMMECOURT.	SJK
HEBUTERNE	14.9.15	—	4th. Battery registered targets on SERRE Front.	SJK
HEBUTERNE	15.9.15	—	HEBUTERNE shelled. 5th. Battery retaliated on GOMMECOURT.	SJK
HEBUTERNE	16.9.15	—	Colonel and Adjutant attended C.R.A's Conference. Wireless installed near Brigade Headquarters.	SJK

WAR DIARY
or
INTELLIGENCE SUMMARY.

Army Form C. 2118.

Place	Date	Hour	Summary of Events and Information	Remarks and references to Appendices
HEBUTERNE	17-9-15		HEBUTERNE shelled in the afternoon; 5th Battery replied on GOMMECOURT.	EJK
HEBUTERNE	18-9-15		Obtained extra billets for the wagon lines in ST. LEGER. 5th Battery fired in conjunction with an aeroplane.	EJK
HEBUTERNE	19-9-15		Voluntary service at Brigade Headquarters.	EJK
HEBUTERNE	20-9-15		The replenishment of ammunition was practised.	EJK
HEBUTERNE	21-9-15		The C.R.A. held a conference which the Colonel and Adjutant attended. Villages and second line trenches are to be shelled in future in preference to front line trenches. We shelled GOMMECOURT in the afternoon and the Germans retaliated on HEBUTERNE.	EJK
HEBUTERNE	22-9-15		Nothing to report.	EJK
HEBUTERNE	23-9-15		Colonel and Adjutant attended a conference of the G.O.C. R.A. in the morning. Final orders received for a three day bombardment of the German lines, which began at 3pm. We shelled front line trenches and redoubt in GOMMECOURT Wood at 3.6.m. and at 5.p.m. we shelled GOMMECOURT Village and a machine-gun emplacement.	EJK

WAR DIARY
or
INTELLIGENCE SUMMARY.
(Erase heading not required.)

Army Form C. 2118.

Place	Date	Hour	Summary of Events and Information	Remarks and references to Appendices
	23-9-15 Cont'd		100 rounds were fired in all. The German artillery replied on our front line trenches, but did not shell our gun positions.	RK
HEBUTERNE	24-9-15		German lines were bombarded at 2.0 p.m. and 5.0 p.m. 4th and 5th Batteries shelled German front line trenches and 4th Battery shelled LA LOUVIERE Farm, and 5th Battery RETTENOY Farm and GOMMECOURT. The Germans made no reply.	RK
HEBUTERNE	25-9-15		We bombarded again at 2.30 p.m. and 5.30 p.m. Same points in front line were shelled, and same villages and farms as yesterday. Fire appeared to be effective.	RK
HEBUTERNE	26-9-15		We fired at German front line trenches and also fired at a Battery with aeroplane observation. Whole procedure of aeroplane very slow.	RK
HEBUTERNE	27-9-15		Orders were received not to expend any ammunition. Front very quiet. We did not fire.	RK
HEBUTERNE	28-9-15		Front very quiet. We did not fire.	RK
HEBUTERNE	29-9-15		Front very quiet. We did not fire.	RK
HEBUTERNE	30-9-15		Nothing to report. Front extremely quiet.	RK

12/7308

48th Battalion

4th S.M. Bde R. & A.

pt VII

Oct 15

CONFIDENTIAL.

WAR DIARY

of

1/4th. Sth. Mid. Field Artillery Brigade, (How).

From October 1st. 1915 To October 31st. 1915.

(Volume 15).

H West LT., COL.
1/4th. S.M. FIELD ARTY. BDE. (HOW)

To/ Officer i/c A. G's Office,
   BASE.

Army Form C. 2118.

WAR DIARY
or
INTELLIGENCE SUMMARY.
(Erase heading not required.)

Instructions regarding War Diaries and Intelligence Summaries are contained in F. S. Regs., Part II. and the Staff Manual respectively. Title pages will be prepared in manuscript.

Place	Date	Hour	Summary of Events and Information	Remarks and references to Appendices
HEBUTERNE	1.10.15	-	Situation very quiet. Capt. Kidd left for duty with 15th Division. Lieut. J. H. Leather appointed Acting Adjutant.	JW
HEBUTERNE	2.10.15	-	4th and 5th Battery's started work on reserve gun pits behind SAILLY. Nothing further to report.	JW
HEBUTERNE	3.10.15		4th and 5th Battery's fired at machine-gun emplacements North and South of CHEMIN CREUX, with good results. Observation in valley difficult owing to mist.	JW
HEBUTERNE	4.10.15		Enemy shelled FONQUEVILLERS. 5th Battery retaliated on GOMMECOURT, and RETTENOY FARM.	JW
HEBUTERNE	5.10.15		Trench mortar observed in action North of Point 301.	JW
HEBUTERNE	6.10.15		The enemy began a very violent rifle and machine-gun fire at 7.45 p.m. all along the HEBUTERNE Front. 4th and 5th Battery's replied at 10.15 p.m. on Points 862, 863 and 349.	JW
HEBUTERNE	7.10.15	-	Nothing to report.	JW
HEBUTERNE	8.10.15		Trench Mortar shelled our trenches from Point 347 at 9.40 p.m. and did considerable damage. 5th Battery retaliated on	JW

WAR DIARY
or
INTELLIGENCE SUMMARY.

(Erase heading not required.)

Army Form C. 2118

Place	Date	Hour	Summary of Events and Information	Remarks and references to Appendices
	8-10-15 Cont'd	-	Points 347 and 349, and a wagon was heard galloping away into GOMMECOURT. 5th Battery continue work on the new huts on the FONQUEVILLERS – HEBUTERNE Road.	S/W
HEBUTERNE	9.10.15.		Situation quiet on our front. French Mortars heard South of us, in the 4th Division.	S/W
HEBUTERNE	10-10-15	-	5th Battery engaged machine gun in action in front of GOMMECOURT Wood. Germans very active on 2nd lines.	S/W
HEBUTERNE	11.10.15	-	Nothing to report.	S/W
HEBUTERNE	12-10-15	-	Divisional Artillery demonstration on forts and machine gun positions on the Western edge of GOMMECOURT Wood. Several machine guns silenced. Enemy retaliated heavily on FONQUEVILLERS. 4th Battery registered Point 863 from their new position in the orchard. Details sent to cut timber in WARNIMONT Wood for reserve positions, and horse standings.	S/W
HEBUTERNE	13.10.15	-		S/W
HEBUTERNE	14-10-15	-	Situation quiet. 4th Battery registered their night-lines with the section lately moved into the orchard.	S/W
HEBUTERNE	15-10-15		Nothing to report.	S/W
HEBUTERNE	16.10.15		4th Battery in co-operation with 1st Brigade shelled Point 301 and	S/W

Army Form C. 2118

WAR DIARY
or
INTELLIGENCE SUMMARY.
(Erase heading not required.)

Instructions regarding War Diaries and Intelligence Summaries are contained in F. S. Regs., Part II. and the Staff Manual respectively. Title pages will be prepared in manuscript.

Place	Date	Hour	Summary of Events and Information	Remarks and references to Appendices
	16.10.15	Cont.d	surrounding trenches. The day was misty and observation difficult.	
HEBUTERNE	17.10.15		MINENWERFER in action near GOMMECOURT Church. 5th Battery fired a few rounds in the morning and silenced it for the time being. They were compelled to fire again in the afternoon, the MINENWERFER having moved some 200 yards more South. No material damage was done to our trenches.	SW
HEBUTERNE	18-10-15		MINENWERFER again troublesome, at intervals during the day, both in GOMMECOURT Wood and to the South of our Divisional Area. From 2.+5 p.m. to 3.+5 p.m., the Germans shelled HEBUTERNE very heavily; and SAILLY with incendiary shells. Divisional artillery combined with 4th Division on points 863, 301 and South. Germans replied very heavily on our trenches opposite. Night was quiet, and repair work uninterrupted. Aeroplanes report a series of black objects all along the parapets of the German trenches from GOMMECOURT Southwards.	SW
HEBUTERNE	19.10.15		Very quiet except for MINENWERFERS which were again in action, in GOMMECOURT Wood and Point 374. 4th Battery fired on	SW

1577 Wt.W10791/1773 500,000 1/15 D. D. & L.   A.D.S.S./Forms/C. 2118.

WAR DIARY
or
INTELLIGENCE SUMMARY.
(Erase heading not required.)

Army Form C. 2118

Place	Date	Hour	Summary of Events and Information	Remarks and references to Appendices
	19-10-15 Contd.		the latter, silencing it.	
HEBUTERNE	20-10-15		Sh. Battery right section moved into new positions on the FONQUEVILLERS Road.	J.W.
HEBUTERNE	21-10-15		Sh. Battery registered two or three targets from their new position. Otherwise very quiet.	J.W.
HEBUTERNE	22-10-15		4.K. Battery fired at and silenced a hostile trench Mortar, in action near Point 374.	J.W.
HEBUTERNE	23-10-15		Divisional Artillery combined against the trenches from Point 863 to Point 301 with good effect. Enemy did not retaliate.	J.W.
HEBUTERNE	24-10-15		Nothing to report.	J.W.
HEBUTERNE	25-10-15		Nothing to report.	J.W.
HEBUTERNE	26-10-15		Nothing to report.	J.W.
HEBUTERNE	27-10-15		Sh. Battery fired at a new fortification in northern part of GOMMECOURT WOOD.	J.W.
HEBUTERNE	28-10-15		Enemy artillery rather more active.	J.W.

Army Form C. 2118

WAR DIARY
or
INTELLIGENCE SUMMARY.
(Erase heading not required.)

Place	Date	Hour	Summary of Events and Information	Remarks and references to Appendices
HEBUTERNE	29-10-15		Divisional Artillery had a combined bombardment on enemy 2nd line trenches. Orders received that the 5th Battery are to retaliate on GOMMECOURT whenever the enemy shell HEBUTERNE.	FW
HEBUTERNE	30-10-15		Enemy fired a few shell into HEBUTERNE. 5th Battery retaliated on GOMMECOURT.	FW
HEBUTERNE	31-10-15		5th Battery again retaliated on GOMMECOURT. 4th Battery fired on a new front line trench, constructed by the enemy on the extreme right of the Divisional Line.	FW

48th Division

D/7636

1/4th St. Bde. R.F.A.

Nov. 1915

Vol VIII

Army Form C. 2118.

WAR DIARY
or
INTELLIGENCE SUMMARY.
(Erase heading not required.)

Place	Date	Hour	Summary of Events and Information	Remarks and references to Appendices
HEBUTERNE	1-11-15	—	5h. Battery shelled GOMMECOURT in retaliation for the shelling of HEBUTERNE.	J.M.K
HEBUTERNE	2-11-15		5h. Battery fired a few rounds into GOMMECOURT in retaliation for shelling of HEBUTERNE, and also searched for a minenwerfer firing from the direction of GOMMECOURT WOOD.	J.M.K
HEBUTERNE	3-11-15		5th Battery retaliated on GOMMECOURT for shelling of HEBUTERNE.	W.R.T.W
HEBUTERNE	4-11-15		Nothing to record.	W.R.T.W
HEBUTERNE	5-11-15		Preliminary bombardment by the 48th Divisional Artillery of the enemy's front line trenches from the right of our line to North of the CHEMIN CREUX. The 4th Brigade fired at a rapid rate to along 2nd line trench where having dug outs had been located owing to smoke having advanced observa.	W.R.T.W
HEBUTERNE	6-11-15		Nothing to record	J.M.K
HEBUTERNE	7-11-15		5th Battery fired at front line trenches round edge of GOMMECOURT WOOD.	J.M.K
HEBUTERNE	8-11-15		4th Battery experimented with the first issue of 40lb H.E. Shell which O.C. was charged of a maximum range of about 6000 yds. Owing to fuse the maximum range of two rounds	J.M.K

WAR DIARY
or
INTELLIGENCE SUMMARY.

(Erase heading not required.)

Army Form C. 2118.

Place	Date	Hour	Summary of Events and Information	Remarks and references to Appendices
	8/11/15 cont.		Tried, but good results were obtained at 2000, 3000 & 4700 yds. The range card proved reliable. The bursts were good though a little early. Less than N°7, the gun did not jump in the air but ran back smoothly. There was no smoke but the first appeared to be longer & the heat stronger. Two rivulets were noted on LA LOUVIERE FERME from the range card reading. Enemy shelled HEBUTERNE by Reg & 5th Bty retaliated on GOMMECOURT. The 4th Brigade were made responsible for the counter attack. 2/Lt F. MOTTRAM was detailed as Acting GARRISON QUARTERMASTER for this duty.	1.M.L.
9/11/15 HEBUTERNE			40 U. Shells were lobbed at the maximum range & tried factory up to about 6000 yards. The enemy shelled HEBUTERNE in the afternoon and 5th Battery retaliated on GOMMECOURT.	1.M.L.
HEBUTERNE	10.11.15		Nothing to record.	1.M.L.

WAR DIARY or INTELLIGENCE SUMMARY

Army Form C. 2118.

(Erase heading not required.)

Place	Date	Hour	Summary of Events and Information	Remarks and references to Appendices
HEBUTERNE	12.11.15		5th Battery registered front line trench in front of FERME SANS NOM from their new position R. Sec.	
			The weather has been very bad during the past few days. Trenches are falling in and caving in everywhere, on account of the rain. All dugouts found to be in water, planks and material had been placed on the top of corrugated iron sheets at the bottom of the trenches specially to hold the water but (with water army so now adopted) and overhead cover other than corrugated iron is almost useless.	I.A.L.
HEBUTERNE	12.11.15		145th Infantry Bde relieved the 144th Bde in sector which there was no firing.	I.A.L.
HEBUTERNE	13.11.15		5th Battery Right Section moved from their position between HEBUTERNE and FONQUEVILLERS back to their old position behind HEBUTERNE, as owing to insufficient roofing and the heavy rain, their new position was quite untenable. Corrugated iron has been procured for roofing it, and arrange-	

WAR DIARY
or
INTELLIGENCE SUMMARY.

(Erase heading not required.)

Army Form C. 2118.

Place	Date	Hour	Summary of Events and Information	Remarks and references to Appendices
	13/11/15	Cont-d	-ments have been made for proper drainage.	/NK
HEBUTERNE	14.11.15		The Brigade fired 84 rounds in the morning on various points in the enemy's front trenches, such as CHEMIN CREUX and Point 301, doing considerable damage to communication trenches and throwing up large quantities of material. Owing to the wet state of the trenches a shell falling within 20 yards was sufficient to shake in the sides. Enemy retaliated feebly.	/NK
HEBUTERNE	15.11.15		Enemy observed working in their trenches all along the line and appeared to be suffering from flooded trenches. 5th Battery dispersed one party thus engaged.	/NK
HEBUTERNE	16.11.15		Minenwerfer reported in action, by the Infantry, North of GOMMECOURT WOOD. This target was taken on by 5th Battery and result unsatisfactory owing to the inaccurate location of the target by the Infantry.	/NK
HEBUTERNE	17.11.15		Enemy shelled our trenches opposite Point 301 with 15cm howitzers. Small damage was done and the 4.N. Battery retaliated on Point 301.	/NK

Army Form C. 2118.

WAR DIARY
or
INTELLIGENCE SUMMARY.

(Erase heading not required.)

Place	Date	Hour	Summary of Events and Information	Remarks and references to Appendices
HEBUTERNE	18.11.15		Orders received that no more 5" ammunition is to be used until further orders. Lt. Col. West proceeded to England on leave.	I.N.L.
HEBUTERNE	19.11.15		Nothing to report.	I.N.L.
HEBUTERNE	20.11.15		Nothing to report. Too misty to observe.	I.N.L.
HEBUTERNE	21.11.15		Field guns and 6in. howitzers bombarded trenches South East and South of GOMMECOURT with good effect. Enemy appear to be spending a great deal of labour in draining trenches. Pumps are seen at work in GOMMECOURT Wood.	I.N.L.
HEBUTERNE	22.11.15		4th Battery guns to be sent one at a time to SOUASTRE for overhaul. Each gun takes from one to three days as bearings all require re-bushing and pipe boxes filling.	I.N.L.
HEBUTERNE	23.11.15		Nothing to report.	I.N.L.
HEBUTERNE	24.11.15		The 4th Battery came out of action at 5.30pm and went into rest at ARQUEVES. They were relieved in action at 6.30p.m. by the 10th London Battery, R.F.A. (T) 4.5" Q.F. Hows.	I.N.L.

Army Form C. 2118.

WAR DIARY
or
INTELLIGENCE SUMMARY.
(Erase heading not required.)

Instructions regarding War Diaries and Intelligence Summaries are contained in F. S. Regs., Part II. and the Staff Manual respectively. Title pages will be prepared in manuscript.

Place	Date	Hour	Summary of Events and Information	Remarks and references to Appendices
HEBUTERNE	25/11/15		10th London Battery registered LA LOUVIÈRE Farm.	/M.K.
HEBUTERNE	26.11.15		Lt. Col. West returned from leave.	
		1.00am	The Divisional Artillery opened fire on German front line trenches South and South East of GOMMECOURT Wood. After a short bombardment two patrols of fifty men from the 6th. Gloucesters made an attempt to raid the German wire. One party succeeded in getting into the front line trench and captured a large dug-out. Bombing parties proceeded down the side trenches and did considerable execution. The party then retired with one prisoner. Enemy's casualties estimated at not less than forty as against ten of our own. Enemy retaliated on the edge of HEBUTERNE and trenches, but without good effect.	/M.K.
HEBUTERNE	27.11.15		10th London Battery registered their night lines.	
HEBUTERNE	28.11.15	1.30am	Germans shelled our front line trenches and the forward edge of HEBUTERNE Village heavily, with Field Guns and	

Army Form C. 2118.

WAR DIARY
or
INTELLIGENCE SUMMARY.
(Erase heading not required.)

Instructions regarding War Diaries and Intelligence Summaries are contained in F.S. Regs., Part II. and the Staff Manual respectively. Title pages will be prepared in manuscript.

Place	Date	Hour	Summary of Events and Information	Remarks and references to Appendices
	28.11.15 Cont'd		Howitzers for about half an hour, but made no attempt to leave their trenches. Some of the shells used are reported to have contained broken glass. Very little damage was done. Left section of the 10th London Battery exchanged into the gun positions of the 5th Warwick Battery. 5th Battery left section took over the orchard position.	/N.L.
HEBUTERNE	29.11.15			/N.L.
HEBUTERNE	30.11.15		The left section of the 10th London Battery registered the night lines from their position K15 d 7.8. (Sheet 57D N.E. 1/10000). The 4.5" guns in these hits cover a zone only six or seven degrees less than the 5" How".	/N.L.

1577 Wt. W10791/1773 500,000 1/15 D.D. & L. A.D.S.S./Forms/C. 2118.

1/+ in St his Bde R.F.A. (How)

15'

CONFIDENTIAL

WAR DIARY

of

1/4th Sthn Mid. Field Artillery Brigade (Howitzer).

From 1st December, 1915 To 31st December, 1915.

(Volume 17).

J. W. Leather Lt
& ADJT.,
1/4th. S.M. FIELD ARTY., BDE., (HOW)

WAR DIARY
or
INTELLIGENCE SUMMARY.
(Erase heading not required.)

Army Form C. 2118.

Place	Date	Hour	Summary of Events and Information	Remarks and references to Appendices
HEBUTERNE	1/12/15	—	10th London Battery registered CHEMIN CREUX and Point 862.	1.h.
HEBUTERNE	2/12/15	—	1th Battery was inspected in marching order at ARQUEVES by the G.O.C.R.A. 48th Div.	1.h.
HEBUTERNE	3/12/15	—	Overhaul of all guns of the Brigade now completed. Divisional Artillery bombarded CHEMIN CREUX and German third line trenches North of BOIS ROSSIGNOL. 10th London Battery fired with good effect, but the timing of the shrapnel was erratic.	1.h.
HEBUTERNE	4/12/15	—	10th London Battery came out of action and marched to THIEVRES in order to join their Brigade. Owing to the mud and slope of the pits, they took four hours to get clear of the positions.	1.h.
HEBUTERNE	5/12/15	—	4th Battery returned to their position, and the left section 5th Battery returned to their original position.	1.h.
HEBUTERNE	6/12/15	—	Minenwerfer caused great annoyance to the 8th and 6th Staff. wicks, firing from the North of GOMMECOURT. Two mortars appeared to be in action there and twenty rounds were fired on them by the 5th Battery.	1.h.

Army Form C. 2118.

WAR DIARY
or
INTELLIGENCE SUMMARY.
(Erase heading not required.)

Instructions regarding War Diaries and Intelligence Summaries are contained in F.S. Regs., Part II. and the Staff Manual respectively. Title pages will be prepared in manuscript.

Place	Date	Hour	Summary of Events and Information	Remarks and references to Appendices
HEBUTERNE	7/12/5	—	5th Battery fired 23 rounds retaliation on Minenwerfers in action North of GOMMECOURT WOOD.	/Kh
HEBUTERNE	8/12/5		Two minenwerfers appeared to be in action in almost the same place. 5th Battery put thirty odd rounds all round the place from which the puff of smoke and the shell were seen to emerge. The mortar seems to be sunk below the level of the ground and must have a small and very well protected emplacement as our shelling did not seem to have the effect of silencing it. Enemy retaliate more freely now on HEBUTERNE and the other villages, and appears to have one or two more guns and a larger allowance of ammunition than for the past six weeks.	/Kh
HEBUTERNE	9/12/5		5th Battery are now working on their FONQUEVILLERS reserve position with the help of twenty men from the D.A.C. under suggestions from the R.E. Work is very slow owing to the wet and sticky condition of the ground.	/Kh

Army Form C. 2118.

WAR DIARY
or
INTELLIGENCE SUMMARY.
(Erase heading not required.)

Instructions regarding War Diaries and Intelligence Summaries are contained in F.S. Regs., Part II. and the Staff Manual respectively. Title pages will be prepared in manuscript.

Place	Date	Hour	Summary of Events and Information	Remarks and references to Appendices
HEBUTERNE	10/12/15		Nothing to report.	l.H.
HEBUTERNE	11/12/15		5th Battery put out a roving gun at K9a1b near the SAILLY - FONQUEVILLERS road for the purpose of shooting up the minenwerfer which was firing from the North of GOMME COURT Wood.	Sheet 57D 1/20000 TRENCH MAP 9/9/15 l.H.
HEBUTERNE	12/12/15		Registered the Barricade with the roving gun.	l.H.
HEBUTERNE	13/12/15		The 4th Battery right section compelled to leave the orchard position because of the wet weather, and returned to the old French gun pits K15 a 9.4. (Sheet 57D 1/10000). Twenty R.E. Sappers in charge of an officer started to assist 5th Battery on their FONQUEVILLERS position.	l.H.
HEBUTERNE	14/12/15		Nothing to report.	l.H.
HEBUTERNE	15/12/15		Two Minenwerfers have been in action up and down GOMMECOURT for the last two or three days.	l.H.
HEBUTERNE	16/12/15		Too misty to observe	l.H.
HEBUTERNE	17/12/15		Bombardment took place on trenches North and South of	l.H.

T2134. Wt. W708-776. 500000. 4/15. Sir J.C. & S.

Army Form C. 2118.

WAR DIARY
or
INTELLIGENCE SUMMARY.
(Erase heading not required.)

Instructions regarding War Diaries and Intelligence Summaries are contained in F.S. Regs., Part II. and the Staff Manual respectively. Title pages will be prepared in manuscript.

Place	Date	Hour	Summary of Events and Information	Remarks and references to Appendices
	17/12/15	Cont'd	GOMMECOURT, particular attention being paid to enfilading by the Roving Guns of the Division but for the purpose. Enemy retaliated feebly, but later in the evening put a few shells into HEBUTERNE, at intervals of about an hour.	
HEBUTERNE	18/12/15		Nothing to report.	1/15. 1/15.
HEBUTERNE	19/12/15		4th Battery fired on trenches West of LOUVIÈRE with good effect. 5th Battery retaliated on South West corner of GOMMECOURT Wood for Minenwerfer firing.	1/15. 1/15.
HEBUTERNE	20/12/15		Nothing to report.	
HEBUTERNE	21/12/15		Minenwerfer active, retaliated on by 5th Battery.	1/15. 1/15.
HEBUTERNE	22/12/15		Infantry changing. Very misty. Nothing to report.	
HEBUTERNE	23/12/15		Divisional Artillery and 37th Divisional Artillery had a demonstration on Northern edge of GOMMECOURT and the trenches round CHEMIN CREUX. Enemy retaliated more vigorously than they have done for some time, on the	1/15. 1/15.

Army Form C. 2118.

WAR DIARY
or
INTELLIGENCE SUMMARY.
(Erase heading not required.)

Instructions regarding War Diaries and Intelligence
Summaries are contained in F.S. Regs., Part II
and the Staff Manual respectively. Title pages
will be prepared in manuscript.

Place	Date	Hour	Summary of Events and Information	Remarks and references to Appendices
	23/12/15 Cont'd		front trenches and observing stations.	1/16 1/17.
HEBUTERNE	24/12/15		Nothing to report	
HEBUTERNE	25/12/15		Strict injunctions issued against making or receiving any overtures from the enemy. An extra allowance of 300 rounds per gun the 26th was expended on conspicuous points in the enemy front line. In retaliation for enemy firing on SAILLY, 4th Battery fired 40 rounds of 40# shell into PUISIEUX after dusk.	1/17.
HEBUTERNE	26/12/15		5th Battery roving gun brought back to its position between HEBUTERNE and FONQUEVILLERS. One of these positions is now made invisible by covering the pit and ramp with corrugated iron, walls being revetted with sand bags and corrugated iron. The other pit is nearing completion, when the other gun will be brought into it. 4th Battery fired on Point 863 in the morning.	1/17.
HEBUTERNE	27/12/15		In the afternoon 5th Battery retaliated on M.G. emplacement in	

Army Form C. 2118.

WAR DIARY
or
INTELLIGENCE SUMMARY.
(Erase heading not required.)

Instructions regarding War Diaries and Intelligence Summaries are contained in F.S. Regs., Part II. and the Staff Manual respectively. Title pages will be prepared in manuscript.

Place	Date	Hour	Summary of Events and Information	Remarks and references to Appendices
	27/12/15 Cont'd		GOMMECOURT WOOD. Six hostile aeroplanes passed over and dropped lights on the village. Divisional enemy artillery shelled AUTHIE, but did no damage.	/A.T.
HEBUTERNE	28/12/15		Infantry changing. Nothing to report.	/A.T.
HEBUTERNE	29/12/15		Both Batteries registered fresh targets with 4.5" shell for the following day's bombardment.	/A.T.
HEBUTERNE	30/12/15	3.0 p.m	Divisional Artillery held a practice in lifting fire from front line to 2nd line to 3rd line trenches, or the trenches North and South of CHEMIN CREUX. The intention was also to mislead the enemy into expecting an attack. Considerable damage was done to the enemy front line. They replied by making a barrage on our communication trenches and by several unsuccessful attempts to search for our guns.	/A.T.

48

1/4 S M Rae R.F.A.
Jan
W.O XIE

Army Form C. 2118.

WAR DIARY
or
INTELLIGENCE SUMMARY.
(Erase heading not required.)

Instructions regarding War Diaries and Intelligence Summaries are contained in F.S. Regs., Part II. and the Staff Manual respectively. Title pages will be prepared in manuscript.

Place	Date	Hour	Summary of Events and Information	Remarks and references to Appendices
HEBUTERNE	1/4/16	-	Nothing to report.	J.M.R.
dEBUTERNE	2/4/16	-	Both guns of the 5th Battery right section in position on the plain between FONQUEVILLERS and HEBUTERNE. 5th Battery fired on Minenwerfer in afternoon, in GOMME- COURT WOOD. Infantry report direct hit obtained.	J.M.R.
HEBUTERNE	3/4/16		Enemy bombarded our trenches in A sector very heavily in the 8 Kerman while the Infantry were changing. 4th Battery retaliated with 80 rounds on second line trenches immediately opposite.	J.M.R.
HEBUTERNE	4/4/16		Nothing to report.	
HEBUTERNE	5/4/16		Minenwerfers very active in GOMMECOURT wood. 5th Battery fired about 80 rounds and claimed have hit in this place occupied by one of them, but these appear to have been at least two, and possibly three, Minenwerfers in action, and it is impossible to cope with all of them from one observing station.	J.M.R.

Place	Date	Hour	Summary of Events and Information	Remarks and references to Appendices
HEBUTERNE	6/4/16	-	Brigade re-armed with 4.5" Q.F. Howitzers. Team proceeded to DOULLENS in the morning and drew the guns and equipment. One section of each Battery came up the same night and relieved the two Orchard sections.	I.T.R.
HEBUTERNE	7/4/16	-	No. 7 Dial Sight arrived and were fitted and the guns put into working order.	I.T.R.
HEBUTERNE	8/4/16	9.0 a.m	To Monrinuepon North of GOMMECOURT WOOD was drawn by one of our trench mortars. As soon as the Minenwerfer opened fire the 8 inch fired on the emplacement and the 5th Battery Right Section fired 40 rounds into front line trenches just in front. Minenwerfer fired 6 rounds and then ceased fire.	I.T.R.
HEBUTERNE	9/4/16	-	Both Batteries registered with the 4.5" how. The guns were accurately though the drill to fow was slow. Only a lot of charge could be used at no range cards were available.	I.T.R.
HEBUTERNE	10/4/16		Night lines were registered with the 4.5" guns.	I.T.R.

Place	Date	Hour	Summary of Events and Information	Remarks and references to Appendices
HEBUTERNE	11/1/16	—	No firing as Infantry were changing.	
HEBUTERNE	12/1/16	—	Both remaining sections of 5" How. taken out of action and the new guns were brought into action fit.	I.H.L.
HEBUTERNE	13/1/16		Bombardment by Divisional Artillery in the morning on the trenches North of GONNECOURT and round the Barricade on FONQUEVILLERS — GOMMECOURT Road. Enemy retaliated with 90 to 100 rounds from Field Guns, 4th Battery fought eight 5" B.L. How, registered all their night lines including the eight G.S. wagons and all equipment including the Anm. Ork. were taken to DOULLENS for despatch to the Base.	I.H.L.
HEBUTERNE	14/1/16		Nothing to report. D gun of the 5th Battery was sent to the I.O.M. in evening of	I.H.L.
HEBUTERNE	15/1/16		D gun of the 5th Battery was sent to the I.O.M. in evening of the looking gear and was returned the same night.	I.H.L.
HEBUTERNE	16/1/16		5th Battery registered BOIS ROSSIGNOL and LA LOUVIÈRE	I.H.L.
HEBUTERNE	17/1/16		Hostile aeroplane flew over in morning and dropped four	

Army Form C. 2118.

WAR DIARY
or
INTELLIGENCE SUMMARY.
(Erase heading not required.)

Instructions regarding War Diaries and Intelligence Summaries are contained in F. S. Regs., Part II. and the Staff Manual respectively. Title pages will be prepared in manuscript.

Place	Date	Hour	Summary of Events and Information	Remarks and references to Appendices
17/4/16 Bank	—	—	Bombs just North of HEBUTERNE, but did no damage.	/A.2
HEBUTERNE	18/4/16	—	Nothing to report.	/A.2
HEBUTERNE	19/4/16	—	Minenwerfer North of GOMMECOURT Wood was active at 1.30 a.m. in the morning and at 11 p.m. at night, and shelled the Warwick trenches. 5th Battery fired on the German front line trenches.	/A.2 /A.2
HEBUTERNE	20/4/16	—	Nothing to report.	
HEBUTERNE	21/4/16	—	Infantry changing. Normal inspection by A.C. Brigade.	
HEBUTERNE	22/4/16	—	Bombardment by Divisional Artillery of trenches along the South of GOMMECOURT Wood and dug-outs and trenches North of the CHEMIN CREUX N.11. Very considerable damage was done. 5th Battery fired at night on their targets at various intervals. They also experimented with nitro cellulose flameless cartridges and found them very satisfactory for night shooting. The enemy appeared to resent the firing of nights and replied fairly quickly with	

Army Form C. 2118.

WAR DIARY
or
INTELLIGENCE SUMMARY.
(Erase heading not required.)

Place	Date	Hour	Summary of Events and Information	Remarks and references to Appendices
22/4/16 Cont'd		15 am	Hour on various points in the line.	M.L. / M.L. / M.L.
HEBUTERNE	23/4/16	–	Nothing to report.	
HEBUTERNE	24/4/16	–	Nothing to report.	
HEBUTERNE	25/4/16	–	From 2.0 am to 2.4.5 am the enemy sent short shell fire from Field Gun 4.2" and 5.9" Howitzers and Trench Mortars on our trenches running round the North and East of GOMMECOURT WOOD. A patrol succeeded in capturing a machine gun and a man in the wire and restoring a machine gun and two rifles from the sentry post just North of the Barricade on the FONQUEVILLERS – GOMMECOURT Rd. These appeared to be about four men sentry iron stunned by shell fire but no one was actually seen. 5h Battery and Field Guns replied on the trenches along the edge of GOMMECOURT WOOD.	
HEBUTERNE	26/4/16	–	5h Battery fired at a machine-gun emplacement North of the CHEMIN CREUX and damaged the trenches Nth.	M.L.

Place	Date	Hour	Summary of Events and Information	Remarks and references to Appendices
	26/1/16 Cont'd	-	without destroying the slit.	/1.T.R.
HEBUTERNE	27/1/16	-	Infantry changing. No firing. Alarm of gas at 7.30 p.m. which turned out to be false.	/1.T.R.
HEBUTERNE	28/1/16	-	Capt M.G & FIELD took over temporary command of 5th Warwick Battery for a fortnight and Major C.P.NICKALS of the Brigade Ammunition Column.	/1.T.R.
HEBUTERNE	29/1/16		Nothing to report.	/1.T.R.
HEBUTERNE	30/1/16	10.40 a.m	After a short bombardment of four minutes by our Artillery the 5th Warwicks and 6th Gloucesters attempted to cut the enemy wire by hand and penetrate the south-West corner of GOMMECOURT Wood. A similar attempt was made by the 7th Worcesters South of the CHEMIN CREUX. Both attempts were unsuccessful owing to the very thick mist in the valley and to the "concertina wire", which our men had had no experience in cutting. The artillery bombardment on the second line was successfully	" "

Army Form C. 2118.

WAR DIARY
or
INTELLIGENCE SUMMARY.
(Erase heading not required.)

Instructions regarding War Diaries and Intelligence Summaries are contained in F. S. Regs., Part II. and the Staff Manual respectively. Title pages will be prepared in manuscript.

Place	Date	Hour	Summary of Events and Information	Remarks and references to Appendices
	30/4/16 Cont⁴		carried out. The enemy retaliated slightly on the front trenches. Casualties negligible.	I.T.R.
HEBUTERNE	31/4/16	–	Enemy fired a few rounds into HEBUTERNE. Two 77mm shells hit the 4th Battery telephonists billet killing one man and wounding another.	I.T.R. Appendix I Summary of work done by 2nd Warwick (Ho.) Battery during its attachment to 14th R.F.A. Brigade, from 6/4/15 to 20/6/15 is attached hereto.

CONFIDENTIAL.

APPENDIX I.

To

WAR DIARY
(Volume 18).

of

1/4th Sth. Mid. Field Artillery Brigade (Howitzer).

Summary of work done by 4th Warwick (How) Battery during its
attachment to 14th Field Artillery Brigade, from 6th April, 1915
to 20th June, 1915.

By

Major C.FOWLER
and
Captain M.C.FIELD.

CONFIDENTIAL.

Army Form C. 2118.

WAR DIARY
or
INTELLIGENCE SUMMARY.
(Erase heading not required.)

Place	Date	Hour	Summary of Events and Information	Remarks and references to Appendices
	6.4.15	—	On Tuesday the 6th. April, the left section, under Capt. Field and Lieut. Hayes, was attached to the 14th. Brigade R.F.A., commanded by Colonel (now Brig. Genl.) Rous-Johnson. The Brigade then consisted of the 68th and 88th Batteries, R.F.A., one Battery being detached and in another part of the line. The section moved into position at a farm near the Convent at LE BIZET on Tuesday night, and started firing on the following morning. Telephone lines were taken over from the North Midland Howitzer section; also some of their lines for registration purposes, but not their ranges. Observation was from house in LE TOUQUET. The trenches were occupied by the Kings Own and the Lancs. Fusiliers, and on the left by the Monmouths (7). No guns on our right flank and practically no trenches owing to the low flooded land along the River LYS. The 18 pdrs. were on the left flank, and heavies behind.	M.S.7.

Army Form C. 2118.

WAR DIARY
or
INTELLIGENCE SUMMARY.
(Erase heading not required.)

Instructions regarding War Diaries and Intelligence Summaries are contained in F. S. Regs., Part II. and the Staff Manual respectively. Title pages will be prepared in manuscript.

Place	Date	Hour	Summary of Events and Information	Remarks and references to Appendices
	10.4.15	—	At one time more artillery was brought up with a view to a probable push, which however did not come off owing to attacks at YPRES. On Friday the 10th, the section took part in a demonstration when a mine was blown up in the forward houses of LE TOUQUET, firing some 40 rounds at the road running from FRELINGHIEN to LE TOUQUET at 5.30 a.m. The mine was very successful and on this occasion the shooting was good. On the following day the enemy retaliated, firing	m.s.?
	11.4.15	—	5.9 in. howitzers in salvos. One of these was a direct hit on the little shed where the telephone was kept and Bombardier T. HICKMAN was killed. This was the first casualty in the Brigade. During the period the section was in this position a lot of work was done to the pits and platforms, and new wires were laid out under the supervision of Lieut. M.S. Hayes. Gunner Pearsall	m.s.?

Army Form C. 2118.

WAR DIARY
or
INTELLIGENCE SUMMARY.
(Erase heading not required.)

Instructions regarding War Diaries and Intelligence Summaries are contained in F. S. Regs., Part II. and the Staff Manual respectively. Title pages will be prepared in manuscript.

Place	Date	Hour	Summary of Events and Information	Remarks and references to Appendices
			did good work on the lines. At first Captain Field did nearly all the observation, but later on he and Lieut. Hayes took it in reliefs. Visual signalling was arranged but not used. On two occasions only did shells fall near the position, and no harm was done. The principal targets were the Bridge at FRELINGHEIN, the road from the Bridge to LE TOUQUET and trenches in the direction of PONT ROUGE, known as the TRIANGLE. On one occasion the guns set Pond House on fire and exploded some ammunition. The best shooting was at the Triangle.	

Army Form C. 2118.

WAR DIARY
or
INTELLIGENCE SUMMARY.
(Erase heading not required.)

Instructions regarding War Diaries and Intelligence Summaries are contained in F. S. Regs., Part II. and the Staff Manual respectively. Title pages will be prepared in manuscript.

Place	Date	Hour	Summary of Events and Information	Remarks and references to Appendices
LE BIZET	22/4/15		Fired 8 rounds into ERQUINGHEM. Worked on gun pits.	Cf.
	25/4/15		Wagon line moved to PONT NIEPPE. Still working on gun pits.	Cf.
	29/4/15		Fired 8 rounds on fortified wall. About to report to 11th Brigade for orders.	Cf.
	10/5/15		Enemy shelled ARMENTIERES – about 600 rounds.	Cf.
	9/5/15	4.30 a.m.	Demonstration fired 41 rounds at Triangle and Twin Cottages. Mine fired by Infantry.	Cf.
	10/5/15		Gun drill by telephone. German Aeroplane brought down near HOUPLINES.	Cf.
	11/5/15		Fired 9 rounds. New respirators issued. Inspection of iron rations &c.	Cf.
	13/5/15		Called up at 4.40 a.m. by Infantry. Fired 9 rounds on night line. Ammunition shelled in early morning. Fired at Bell Tower House in retaliation for German shelling HOUPLINES.	Cf.
	16/5/15			Cf.
	18/6/15		New type of smoke behind guns out. Mine went off at 7.30 p.m.	Cf.

Army Form C. 2118.

WAR DIARY
or
INTELLIGENCE SUMMARY.
(Erase heading not required.)

Place	Date	Hour	Summary of Events and Information	Remarks and references to Appendices
LE BIZET	16/6/15		Col. H. Shaw was very effectively accompanied by 22 men & by us.	Cf.
	20/6/15		Received orders to "District" overhead cover for guns. Next day orders came to move to PLOEGSTEERT. Left LE BIZET at informed arrival at PLOEGSTEERT at 1.30 a.m.	Cf.

CONFIDENTIAL

WAR DIARY

of

1/4th Sth. Mid. Field Artillery Brigade (Howitzer).

From 1st February, 1916 To 29th February, 1916.

(Volume I9). XI2

J. W. Leather
Lt. & Adjt.
1/4 S. Mid. Field Arty. Bge. (How.)

WAR DIARY
or
INTELLIGENCE SUMMARY.
(Erase heading not required.)

Army Form C. 2118.

Place	Date	Hour	Summary of Events and Information	Remarks and references to Appendices
HEBUTERNE	1/2/16	-	5th Battery and 2nd S.M. Brigade bombarded trenches North of GOMMECOURT.	/.R.
HEBUTERNE	2/2/16	-	Nothing to report.	/.R.
HEBUTERNE	3/2/16	-	Nothing to report.	/.R.
HEBUTERNE	4/2/16	-	5th Battery bombarded second line trenches. Later in the afternoon 5th Battery observing officer saw a working party on a trench mortar emplacement on the Southern edge of GOMMECOURT Wood and dealt with it successfully.	/.R.
HEBUTERNE	5/2/16	-	Enemy fired two or five battery salvos into HEBUTERNE in the afternoon but did no damage. 4th Battery replied on SERRE.	/.R.
HEBUTERNE	6/2/16	-	4th and 5th Batteries fired at working parties and also replied on SERRE for the shelling of HEBUTERNE.	/.R.
HEBUTERNE	7/2/16	-	4th Battery bombarded dug-outs opposite our right Battalion and 5th Battery fired on machine gun emplacements South West of Farm SANS NOM.	/.R.W.

WAR DIARY
or
INTELLIGENCE SUMMARY

Army Form C. 2118.

Place	Date	Hour	Summary of Events and Information	Remarks and references to Appendices
	9/2/16 cont'd		5th Battery also fired at a trench mortar which was firing from GOMMECOURT PARK. "D" Battery of the 184th Brigade taken in the establishment of this Brigade and remained in action at BIENVILLERS under the tactical control of the 37th Division. The batteries wagon lines and head of ammunition column joined our horse lines at ST. LEGER.	
HEBUTERNE	9/2/16		Enemy's artillery showed greatly increased activity. HEBUTERNE and SAILLY-AU-BOIS shelled by Field Guns at intervals throughout the day.	K.R.1.W.
HEBUTERNE	9/2/16		Hostile artillery was active on the Divisional front. Several field guns were again firing on this part. In HEBUTERNE during the day. Several Civil killed in the afternoon by enemy's road BY COMMISSARY Country road CHEMIN GREUX.	K.R.1.W.
HEBUTERNE	10/2/16		Hostile artillery again active on HEBUTERNE during the	K.R.1.W.

WAR DIARY
or
INTELLIGENCE SUMMARY.
(Erase heading not required.)

Army Form C. 2118.

Place	Date	Hour	Summary of Events and Information	Remarks and references to Appendices
	10/2/16 cont⁴		morning. At 12.45 p.m. our own artillery bombarded PUISIEUX 4th Battery firing 45 rounds 5th Battery bombarded trenches West of GOMMECOURT Cemetery. A few rounds Howitzer shells fell in HEBUTERNE during the afternoon. 5th Battery fired on Serre - Road East of PUISIEUX with aeroplane observation.	WRTW
HEBUTERNE	11/2/16		Enemy artillery had a short burst of rapid fire on HEBUTERNE and trenches South East of HEBUTERNE at 10.30 a.m. They also fired a few heavy shells into HEBUTERNE in the afternoon. Divisional Artillery bombarded the trenches round GOMMECOURT CEMETERY at 1.30 a.m. 5th Battery firing 20 rounds.	
HEBUTERNE	12/2/16		Enemy artillery and active to the trenches East and South East of HEBUTERNE. Divisional Artillery had a short bombardment about mid-day on the enemy's trenches. 5th Battery registered a target with aeroplane observation	WRTW

Army Form C. 2118.

WAR DIARY
or
INTELLIGENCE SUMMARY.
(Erase heading not required.)

Instructions regarding War Diaries and Intelligence Summaries are contained in F. S. Regs., Part II. and the Staff Manual respectively. Title pages will be prepared in manuscript.

Place	Date	Hour	Summary of Events and Information	Remarks and references to Appendices
HEBUTERNE	13/2/16		Enemy artillery showed less activity than on the previous day except for a heavy burst of fire at 10.0 a.m. on the trenches South East of HEBUTERNE. 5th Battery again fired with excellent observation.	W.R.H.W
HEBUTERNE	14/2/16		Enemy artillery had been registering on HEBUTERNE and neighbouring trenches without hostility. Kept up a slow bombardment on PONTAVERT with trench mortars. Sent out an enquiry as to whether Heavy Artillery should start an enquiry 90 rounds.	W.R.H.W
HEBUTERNE	15/2/16		Hostile artillery was quiet. 5th Battery fired 40 rounds at HQ smith at machine gun emplacement between Nameless Farm and Sunk Road East of HEBUTERNE	W.R.H.W
HEBUTERNE	16/2/16		4th Battery bombarded trench South of the sunk road during the course of the morning.	W.R.H.W
HEBUTERNE	17/2/16		Enemy very quiet during the day.	W.R.H.W
HEBUTERNE	18/2/16		Under cover of a heavy bombardment between 1.30 a.m and	

WAR DIARY or INTELLIGENCE SUMMARY

Army Form C. 2118.

Place	Date	Hour	Summary of Events and Information	Remarks and references to Appendices
18/2/16 Cont.d		2.30 a.m.	A party of the enemy estimated between twenty and thirty rushed a small part of our trench south of the LA BRAYELLE – HANNESCAMPS Road. Twelve of our men were missing after the enemy had retired.	
HEBUTERNE	19/2/16		Enemy shelled the Junon on our right heavily during the evening. 4th Battery replied on trenches in front of SERRE.	1 K.R.
HEBUTERNE	20/2/16		4th Battery fired 150 rounds on W: 2nd and 3rd line trenches West of SERRE, by order of G.O.C. at 6.15 p.m. 5th Battery fired 100 rounds into GOMMECOURT Village at 10.30 p.m. as sounds of movement had been heard there.	1 K.R.
HEBUTERNE	21/2/16		H.R. Battery reprimented successfully with shrapnel.	1 K.R.
HEBUTERNE	22/2/16		Field gun fired 200 rounds on the West of GOMMECOURT Wood at 11.0 p.m. Enemy replied with canister bombs on Warwick trenches. 5th Battery fired 10 rounds into the wood at mid-night.	1 K.R.

WAR DIARY
or
INTELLIGENCE SUMMARY.
(Erase heading not required.)

Place	Date	Hour	Summary of Events and Information	Remarks and references to Appendices
HEBUTERNE	23/2/16	-	Warwicks annoyed by canister bombs in the afternoon fired from GOMMECOURT Wood. 5th Battery fired with shrapnel for the first time. Weather turned much colder and a fall of snow.	/it.k
HEBUTERNE	24/2/16	-	Heavy fall of snow all day. Nothing to report.	/it.k
HEBUTERNE	25/2/16	-	Nothing to report.	/it.k
HEBUTERNE	26/2/16	-	5th Battery fired a few rounds in the morning. Aeroplanes were hors possibly owing to the snow.	/it.k
HEBUTERNE	27/2/16	-	Very quiet.	/it.k
HEBUTERNE	28/2/16	-	Thaw set in. Transport of rations done by horse transport as no lorries were allowed on the road.	/it.k
HEBUTERNE	29/2/16	-	Stray shell burst close to a party of "D" Battery proceeding to civic parade; casualties 1 killed and 1 wounded.	/it.k

CONFIDENTIAL

WAR DIARY

of

1/4th Sth. Mid. Field Artillery Brigade (Howitzer).

From 1st March, 1916 To 31st March, 1916.

(Volume ~~20~~). XIII

Army Form C. 2118.

WAR DIARY
or
INTELLIGENCE SUMMARY.
(Erase heading not required.)

Place	Date	Hour	Summary of Events and Information	Remarks and references to Appendices
HEBUTERNE	1/3/16		"D" Battery withdrew the section in action at BIENVILLERS and halted the two guns at ST. LEGER.	/u.f.
HEBUTERNE	2/3/16		Gunners belonging to the section of "D" Battery out of action, took over the two guns belonging to the 5th Battery, in action on the plain between FONQUEVILLERS and HEBUTERNE. 5th Battery gunners from this section took over the 4th Battery section on the plain at K.14.d.4.0. 5th Battery gunners evacuated this section preparatory to taking over the two guns belonging to 86th Battery in action South of COLINCAMPS. "D" Battery was attached tactically to the 48th Division for the first time. The zone covered by the Brigade is now extended from the Z at E.23.e. to K.35.a. A bombardment was carried out at 4.30 p.m. by Divisional Artillery on 1st and 2nd line trenches K.23.6 and d. (Sheet 57D N.E. 1/10000 2nd Edition)	/u.f.
HEBUTERNE	3/3/16		Nothing to report. This Division now forms part of the 10th Corps.	/u.f.

Army Form C. 2118.

WAR DIARY
OR
INTELLIGENCE SUMMARY.
(Erase heading not required.)

Instructions regarding War Diaries and Intelligence Summaries are contained in F. S. Regs., Part II. and the Staff Manual respectively. Title pages will be prepared in manuscript.

Place	Date	Hour	Summary of Events and Information	Remarks and references to Appendices
HEBUTERNE	4/3/16	—	4th Battery took over at mid-day two guns from the 82th Battery R.F.A. which were in action South of COINCAMPS at Q.6.B. 10.25. The two guns belonging to "D" Battery, parked at ST. LEGER, were handed over to the 82th Battery	/R
HEBUTERNE	5/3/16	—	Very quiet in the morning. In the afternoon enemy shelled battery positions all along the line but their damage was done except on dummy positions. The battery positions of this Brigade were not shelled.	/R
HEBUTERNE	6/3/16	—	4th Battery registered from their new position	/R
HEBUTERNE	7/3/16	—	Nothing to report.	/R
HEBUTERNE	8/3/16	—	Nothing to report.	/R
HEBUTERNE	9/3/16	—	All three batteries commenced work on reserve positions each to both one section.	/R
HEBUTERNE	10/3/16	—	Work was delayed owing to snow on the ground. FONQUEVILLERS was shelled by the afternoon. "D" Battery replied on the trenches in front.	/R

WAR DIARY
or
INTELLIGENCE SUMMARY.
(Erase heading not required.)

Army Form C. 2118.

Place	Date	Hour	Summary of Events and Information	Remarks and references to Appendices
HEBUTERNE	11/3/16	—	Work continued on reserve howitzer. Casualties — 2 slightly wounded by a stray bullet.	/J.R.
HEBUTERNE	12/3/16	—	4th Battery ceased work on the position they were digging in K.2b. (Sheet 57 D NE 1:10,000 2nd Edn.) "D" Battery continued work on their reserve position which will be made to hold a Battery.	/J.R.
HEBUTERNE	13/3/16		Premature by 1st Eastern Battery behind 5th Battery position in K.14.d. Casualties — 1 killed D.A.C. attached 1 wounded 5th Battery.	/J.R.
HEBUTERNE	14/3/16		4th Battery fired at anti-aircraft guns in action successfully causing them to retire hastily. "B" gun of 4th Battery had a premature outside the front of the pit which Jo. 44 fuze, caused by the shell striking a twig of the tree which overhangs the pit. Casualties — 2 wounded. Both these men were inside the pit at the time. Enemy artillery more active	

Army Form C. 2118.

WAR DIARY
or
INTELLIGENCE SUMMARY.
(Erase heading not required.)

Place	Date	Hour	Summary of Events and Information	Remarks and references to Appendices
	14/3/16 Cont'd		than usual on HEBUTERNE and FONQUEVILLERS and on BAYENCOURT. Heavy artillery group retaliated on GOMMECOURT.	
HEBUTERNE	15/3/16		"D" Battery fired on Douvile Farm, which stands north of BUCQUOY, and appears to have been untouched hitherto. Enemy fired on Warwick Trenches with minenwerfers in the early morning. "D" Battery retaliated.	I.A.L.
HEBUTERNE	16/3/16		Nothing to report.	I.A.L. P.A.R.
HEBUTERNE	17/3/16		Enemy artillery very active on HEBUTERNE and FONQUE-VILLERS. 4th Battery replied for bombardment of our trenches at K.23.6. Very successful shoot.	I.A.L.
HEBUTERNE	18/3/16		5th Battery replied on canister mortar firing from south-west corner of GOMMECOURT WOOD. Enemy artillery active during the day.	I.A.L.

Army Form C. 2118.

WAR DIARY
or
INTELLIGENCE SUMMARY.
(Erase heading not required.)

Instructions regarding War Diaries and Intelligence Summaries are contained in F.S. Regs., Part II. and the Staff Manual respectively. Title pages will be prepared in manuscript.

Place	Date	Hour	Summary of Events and Information	Remarks and references to Appendices
HEBUTERNE	19/3/16		Enemy commenced a violent bombardment at 1.55 a.m., lasting about an hour, on trenches in K.17. Field Guns, Howitzers, Minenwerfers and Rifle Grenades took part. Enemy also employed gas shells which upon detonation gave out heavy white fumes which affected the eyes. An enemy aeroplane dropped a green light above the point at midnight. Green flares in pairs were sent up prior to and during the bombardment. A bombing party penetrated our trenches but were repulsed. One prisoner was taken and it is thought that a large number were killed in the enemy wire. Field guns and "D" Battery bombarded GOMMECOURT about 12 o'clock noon.	1.M.L.
HEBUTERNE	20/3/16		Bombardment repeated. Enemy artillery very quiet.	1.M.L.
HEBUTERNE	21/3/16		Nothing to report.	1.M.L.
HEBUTERNE	22/3/16		Very quiet. Division becomes part of 8th Corps.	1.M.L.

Army Form C. 2118.

WAR DIARY
or
INTELLIGENCE SUMMARY.
(Erase heading not required.)

Instructions regarding War Diaries and Intelligence Summaries are contained in F. S. Regs., Part II. and the Staff Manual respectively. Title pages will be prepared in manuscript.

Place	Date	Hour	Summary of Events and Information	Remarks and references to Appendices
HEBUTERNE	23/3/16		A successful enterprise was carried out by the 8th Warwicks on the trenches on the west side of GOMMECOURT Wood. Wire was destroyed by Bangalore torpedoes, and a small party succeeded in entering the enemy trench. Several of the enemy were killed, dug outs were bombed, and one prisoner and several samples of equipment and gas helmets were brought away. Several Artillery fired meanwhile on machine-gun emplacements on either side of the point of entry and on the 2nd line trenches.	
HEBUTERNE	24/3/16		Very quiet. No expenditure of 4.5" ammunition allowed until further orders.	
HEBUTERNE	25/3/16		Nothing to report.	
HEBUTERNE	26/3/16		Nothing to report. No firing.	
HEBUTERNE	27/3/16		An allowance of 10 rounds for the Brigade, per day, was allowed again.	

Army Form C. 2118.

WAR DIARY
or
INTELLIGENCE SUMMARY.
(Erase heading not required.)

Instructions regarding War Diaries and Intelligence Summaries are contained in F. S. Regs., Part II. and the Staff Manual respectively. Title pages will be prepared in manuscript.

Place	Date	Hour	Summary of Events and Information	Remarks and references to Appendices
HEBUTERNE	28/3/16		Nothing to report.	1/T.K
HEBUTERNE	29/3/16		Nothing to report	1/T.K
HEBUTERNE	30/3/16		Enemy showed activity with minenwerfers and carried bombs.	1/T.K
HEBUTERNE	31/3/16		Nothing to report.	1/T.K

CONFIDENTIAL.

WAR DIARY

of

1/4th Sth. Mid. Field Artillery Brigade (Howitzer).

From 1st April, 1916 To 30th April, 1916.

(Volume 21).

Lt. & Adjt.
1/4 S. Mid. Field Arty. Bge. (How.)

WAR DIARY
or
INTELLIGENCE SUMMARY.
(Erase heading not required.)

Army Form C. 2118.

Place	Date	Hour	Summary of Events and Information	Remarks and references to Appendices
HEBUTERNE	1/4/16	–	Nothing to report.	1. P.
HEBUTERNE	2/4/16	–	Nothing to report.	1. K. P.
HEBUTERNE	3/4/16	–	Enemy very quiet except for trench mortars in the evening.	1. P. / 1. H.E.
HEBUTERNE	4/4/16	–	Nothing to report.	1. H.E.
HEBUTERNE	5/4/16	–	Enemy in front of GOMMECOURT appear to echoe themselves more than usual, apparently indicating that a new regiment has taken over.	1. K. P.
HEBUTERNE	6/4/16	9.25p	Violent bombardment was started by the enemy but proved to be far south out of the Divisional Area. Left Section of 4th Battery in Q.2.b. was relieved by a section of C/171 How. Battery, R.F.A., and proceeded to the wagon lines for a rest. The establishment in the Brigade is now changed to 17% shrapnel 83% H.E.	1. H.E.
HEBUTERNE	7/4/16	–	Nothing to report.	1. H.E.
HEBUTERNE	8/4/16	–	Nothing to report.	1. H.E.
HEBUTERNE	9/4/16	–	Nothing to report.	1. K. P.

WAR DIARY
or
INTELLIGENCE SUMMARY.

(Erase heading not required.)

Army Form C. 2118.

Place	Date	Hour	Summary of Events and Information	Remarks and references to Appendices
HEBUTERNE	10/4/16	-	Nothing to report.	J.R.
HEBUTERNE	11/4/16	-	On night 11/12th a new advance trench was dug in front of K sector in K.16.a. by one battalion working all night. This was photographed by a German aeroplane next morning and shelled intermittently all through the following night. 4th Battery had a premature with "B" gun, caused by No. 100 fuze delay action, or a small piece of metal which fell into the muzzle from the rear of the pit. Shell burst about 20 yards in front. Casualties, 1 wounded.	J.R.
HEBUTERNE	12/4/16	-	Wiring drill carried out by 4th Battery section at rest.	J.R.
HEBUTERNE	13/4/16	-	Enemy shelled close to 5th Battery Observing Station. Casualties, 1 wounded with shrapnel. Enemy made two short bombardments on our trenches during the night, but took no further action.	J.R.
HEBUTERNE	14/4/16	-	We retaliated in the same manner at 10.45p.m. and 11.30p.m.	J.R.
HEBUTERNE	15/4/16	-	Nothing to report.	J.R.

Army Form C. 2118.

WAR DIARY
or
INTELLIGENCE SUMMARY.
(Erase heading not required.)

Instructions regarding War Diaries and Intelligence Summaries are contained in F. S. Regs., Part II. and the Staff Manual respectively. Title pages will be prepared in manuscript.

Place	Date	Hour	Summary of Events and Information	Remarks and references to Appendices
HEBUTERNE	16/4/16		"D" Battery fired 40 rounds in a small bombardment on trenches north of GOMMECOURT – FONQUEVILLERS Road.	
HEBUTERNE	17/4/16		Enemy showed activity every night on our new forward trench opposite the CHEMIN CREUX.	
HEBUTERNE	18/4/16		5th Battery replied to this bombardment on two occasions. 5th Battery Right Section went out for a rest, 4th Battery Section came back to their orchard section which had been rebuilt.	
HEBUTERNE	19/4/16		Nothing to report.	
HEBUTERNE	20/4/16		Nothing to report.	
HEBUTERNE	21/4/16		Enemy bombarded new trench heavily in the afternoon. 4th Battery replied on CHEMIN CREUX and trenches opposite, together with the rest of the Divisional Artillery.	
HEBUTERNE	22/4/16		Enemy continued to shell the new trench daily.	
HEBUTERNE	23/4/16		Nothing to report.	
HEBUTERNE	24/4/16		Enemy demonstrated on our front line all along the	

Army Form C. 2118.

WAR DIARY
or
INTELLIGENCE SUMMARY.
(Erase heading not required.)

Instructions regarding War Diaries and Intelligence Summaries are contained in F. S. Regs., Part II. and the Staff Manual respectively. Title pages will be prepared in manuscript.

Place	Date	Hour	Summary of Events and Information	Remarks and references to Appendices
	24/4/16	Cont.d	front of GOMMECOURT with Field Guns and Minenwerfers.	
HEBUTERNE	25/4/16	-	Nothing to report.	
HEBUTERNE	26/4/16	-	Enemy artillery very active along the Divisional front.	
HEBUTERNE	27/4/16	-	Nothing to report.	
HEBUTERNE	28/4/16	-	Enemy bombarded several batteries whose zone is on CHEMIN CREUX and southwards. Trench mortars active in GOMMECOURT WOOD.	
HEBUTERNE	29/4/16	-	Nothing to report.	
HEBUTERNE	30/4/16	-	Enemy unusually quiet except at night when raid was attempted unsuccessfully by Division south of us.	

CONFIDENTIAL.

WAR DIARY

of

243rd Brigade, R. F. A.
(Late 1/4th Sth. Mid. Field Artillery Brigade, Howitzer)

From 1st May, 1916   To 31st May, 1916.
(Volume 22).

Lt. & Adjt.
243 S. Mid. Field Arty. Bge.

Army Form C. 2118.

WAR DIARY
or
INTELLIGENCE SUMMARY.
(Erase heading not required.)

Instructions regarding War Diaries and Intelligence Summaries are contained in F. S. Regs., Part II. and the Staff Manual respectively. Title pages will be prepared in manuscript.

Place	Date	Hour	Summary of Events and Information	Remarks and references to Appendices
HEBUTERNE	1/5/16	-	Nothing to report.	
HEBUTERNE	2/5/16	-	Nothing to report.	
HEBUTERNE	3/5/16	-	Nothing to report.	
HEBUTERNE	4/5/16	-	Nothing to report.	
HEBUTERNE	5/5/16	-	Nothing to report.	
HEBUTERNE	6/5/16	-	5th Divisional Infantry relieved 48th Division in the trenches in front of HEBUTERNE.	M.L.
HEBUTERNE	7/5/16	-	Nothing to report.	M.L.
HEBUTERNE	8/5/16	-	5.R.Battery section at rest came into action in the new position just completed at K.14.d.3.0. 5th Battery Left section came into action in the orchard, where they were relieved by the 10th London Battery and proceeded to the other two pits at K.14.d.3.0. One section "D" Battery between FONQUEVILLERS and HEBUTERNE was relieved by the 10th London Battery, and proceeded to their wagon lines at ST. LEGER.	57 DNF Operation Orders 2nd Feb.
HEBUTERNE	9/5/16			M.L.

WAR DIARY
or
INTELLIGENCE SUMMARY.
(Erase heading not required.)

Army Form C. 2118.

Place	Date	Hour	Summary of Events and Information	Remarks and references to Appendices
HEBUTERNE	10/5/16	—	4th Battery came out of action complete and proceeded to ST. LEGER. Section of "D" Battery in FONQUEVILLERS was relieved by 2nd Sec'y (4th) Battery and proceeded to ST. LEGER.	1 R.E.
ST. LEGER	11/5/16	—	Brigade Head quarters moved from HEBUTERNE to ST. LEGER. 5th Battery was grouped tactically with the 2nd 1st/2nd Mid F.A. Bde.	1 H.E. 1 H.E. 1 H.E. 1 H.E.
ST. LEGER	12/5/16	—	O.O's bathed, flag wagging, and officers ride	
ST. LEGER	13/5/16	—	Nothing to report.	
ST. LEGER	14/5/16	—	Church Parade	
ST. LEGER	15/5/16	—	Officers Ride. The Brigade Ammunition Column was dissolved and the personnel, horses and vehicles divided up amongst 48th Div. Amm. Col. and 1st, 2nd and 3rd Bde. Amm. Columns which henceforth became 1st, 2nd and 3rd Sections of the 48th Div. Amm. Col.	1 H.E.
ST. LEGER	16/5/16	—	Nothing to report.	
ST. LEGER	17/5/16	—	Orders received that the three Howitzer Batteries of the Brigade were to be split up and sent, one to 1st S.M.F.A. Bde, one to	1 H.E.

Army Form C. 2118.

WAR DIARY
or
INTELLIGENCE SUMMARY.
(Erase heading not required.)

Place	Date	Hour	Summary of Events and Information	Remarks and references to Appendices
	17/5/16	Cont.d	2nd S.M.F.A. Bde, and one to 3rd S.M.F.A. Bde. The three 18 pr. Batteries of 1st, 2nd and 3rd Brigades, lately formed, were to form the fourth Brigade under the present Headquarters.	/R
ST. LEGER	18/5/16		Exchange was effected and names of the Artillery Brigade of this Division change to 240th, 241st, 242nd and 243rd Brigade, R.F.A. The Battery became D/240, 5th Battery became D/241, and "D" Battery became D/242. The new batteries of this Brigade became A/243, B/243 and C/243. "B" Battery horse lines at COUIN, "A" and "C" Battery horse lines at ST. LEGER.	/R /L /L /L
ST. LEGER	19/5/16		Nothing to report.	/L
ST. LEGER	20/5/16		"A" and "C" Batteries inspected in marching order by the G.O.C, R.A.	/L /L
ST. LEGER	21/5/16		Church Parade.	/L
ST. LEGER	22/5/16	6.30 am	"B" Battery Marching Order Parade. "A" and "C" Batteries [missing] Briel.	/L

WAR DIARY
or
INTELLIGENCE SUMMARY.
(Erase heading not required.)

Army Form C. 2118.

Place	Date	Hour	Summary of Events and Information	Remarks and references to Appendices
ST. LEGER	23/5/16		Forenoon.- Driving Drill. Evening.- Tactical ride for Officers	
ST. LEGER	24/5/16		Drill orders for Batteries in the morning. Officers lecture in the evening	1/15
ST. LEGER	25/5/16		Battery Staffs. - Signalling classes daily.	1/15
ST. LEGER	26/5/16		Driving Drill. Officers Ride	1/15
ST. LEGER	27/5/16		Parades under battery arrangements	1/15
ST. LEGER	28/5/16		Church Parade for the Divisional Artillery at ST. LEGER, attended by C.R.A.	1/15
ST. LEGER	29/5/16		Driving Drill. "B" Battery in Marching Order.	1/15
ST. LEGER	30/5/16		Driving Drill, teams only, owing to wet weather.	1/15
ST. LEGER	31/5/16		Parades under Battery arrangements. Reconnaissance by O.C. Brigade and Battery Commanders of new positions between MESNIL and AUCHONVILLERS.	1/15

CONFIDENTIAL

WAR DIARY

of

243rd Brigade, R. F. A.

From 1st June, 1916 To 30th June, 1916.

(Volume 23).

[signature]
Lt. & Adjt.
243 S. Mid. Field Arty. Bge.

Army Form C. 2118.

WAR DIARY
or
INTELLIGENCE SUMMARY.
(Erase heading not required.)

Instructions regarding War Diaries and Intelligence Summaries are contained in F. S. Regs., Part II. and the Staff Manual respectively. Title pages will be prepared in manuscript.

Place	Date	Hour	Summary of Events and Information	Remarks and references to Appendices
ST. LEGER	1-6-16	—	Driving drill	1.6.6
ST. LEGER	2-6-16	—	Brigade Route March.	1.6.6
ST. LEGER	3-6-16	—	Driving drill in the morning. Orders given for the relief of the 240th Brigade by the 243rd Brigade, in the command of "A" Group 48th Division. "B" Battery went up into action into K.20.d (Sheet 57.D N= 29000.) & then concurred in the plan south west of HEBUTERNE.	1.6.6
SAILLY-AU-BOIS	4-6-16	—	Relief of 240th Brigade was completed. "A" and "C" Batteries took over from "C" and "B" Batteries 240th Brigade in K.15.c. and K.20.d. D/240 Bn and A/171 Field Coys completed the Group Group front extending from K.17. N.E. 5. K.23.b.	1.6.6
SAILLY-AU-BOIS	5-6-16	—	Nothing to report.	1.6.6
SAILLY-AU-BOIS	6-6-16	—	Hostile activity normal. 143rd Infantry Brigade dug a new trench in front of our line north of the Sucre Park during the night without being much molested.	1.6.6
SAILLY-AU-BOIS	7-6-16	—	Nothing to report.	1.6.6

Army Form C. 2118.

WAR DIARY
or
INTELLIGENCE SUMMARY.

(Erase heading not required.)

Instructions regarding War Diaries and Intelligence Summaries are contained in F. S. Regs., Part II. and the Staff Manual respectively. Title pages will be prepared in manuscript.

Place	Date	Hour	Summary of Events and Information	Remarks and references to Appendices
SAILLY-AU-BOIS	8-6-16	—	A/243 Battery in Battle Position No 5 was shelled by a 5.9" battery early in the morning. One emplacement was hit but not much damaged. Casualties nil.	/u
SAILLY-AU-BOIS	9-6-16	—	D.A.C. commenced to replenish all gun position in use or shortly to be in use up to 1000 rounds per gun 18-pr. and 800 rounds per gun 4.5" How".	/u
SAILLY-AU-BOIS	10-6-16	—	Nothing to report.	/u
SAILLY-AU-BOIS	11-6-16	—	Nothing to report.	/u
SAILLY-AU-BOIS	12-6-16	—	One Battery 242 Bde. relieved A/171 and became part of the Group.	/u
SAILLY-AU-BOIS	13-6-16	—	242 Brigade relieved from command of the Group by 242 Brigade. Brigade Headquarters and Batteries returned to wagon lines at ST LEGER.	/u
ST. LEGER	14-6-16	—	Nothing to report.	/u
ST. LEGER	15-6-16	—	Clock time advanced one hour on night 14/15th by order of French Government. Reconnaissance by Battery Commanders and O.C. Brigade.	/u

Army Form C. 2118.

WAR DIARY
or
INTELLIGENCE SUMMARY.
(Erase heading not required.)

Instructions regarding War Diaries and Intelligence Summaries are contained in F. S. Regs., Part II. and the Staff Manual respectively. Title pages will be prepared in manuscript.

Place	Date	Hour	Summary of Events and Information	Remarks and references to Appendices
ST. LEGER	16-6-16	-	Nothing to report	/ast. C
ST. LEGER	17-6-16	-	Nothing to report	/1 L
ST. LEGER	18-6-16	-	Hostile aircraft very active	/1 L
ST. LEGER	19-6-16	-	Nothing to report	/1 L
ST. LEGER	20-6-16	-	Battery Drill Order.	/1 L
ST. LEGER	21-6-16	-	Battery Drill Order.	/1 L
ST. LEGER	22-6-16	-	Nothing to Report.	/1 L
ST. LEGER	23-6-16	-	Nothing to report. "B" Battery attached to 29th Div and came in action N.E. MESNIL	/15 L
ST. LEGER	24-6-16	-	Bombardment commenced all along the Army front.	/15 L
ST. LEGER	25-6-16	-	Bombardment continued. Enemy Treplied feebly.	/15 L
ST. LEGER	26-6-16	-	Enemy commenced retaliation on villages.	/15 L
ST. LEGER	27-6-16	-	Bombardment continued.	/15 L
ST. LEGER	28-6-16	-	The Brigade less "B" Battery, proceeded to wagon line position behind MAILLY MAILLET with orders to proceed forward on the following morning subsequent to an assault by the Infantry. Operations were postponed owing to wet weather and Brigade	/15 L

Army Form C. 2118.

WAR DIARY
or
INTELLIGENCE SUMMARY.
(Erase heading not required.)

Instructions regarding War Diaries and Intelligence Summaries are contained in F. S. Regs., Part II. and the Staff Manual respectively. Title pages will be prepared in manuscript.

Place	Date	Hour	Summary of Events and Information	Remarks and references to Appendices
	28-6-16	Cont.	returned to ST. LEGER in the evening	
ST. LEGER	29-6-16		Bombardment continued	
ST. LEGER	30-6-16		Brigade returned to wagon line position behind MAILLY MAILLET	

CONFIDENTIAL

WAR DIARY
of
243rd Brigade, R. F. A.

From 1st July, 1916 To 31st July, 1916.
(Volume 24).

F West Lt. Col.
243 S. Mid. Field Arty. Bde.

Army Form C. 2118.

WAR DIARY
or
INTELLIGENCE SUMMARY.
(Erase heading not required.)

Instructions regarding War Diaries and Intelligence Summaries are contained in F.S. Regs, Part II. and the Staff Manual respectively. Title pages will be prepared in manuscript.

Place	Date	Hour	Summary of Events and Information	Remarks and references to Appendices
MAILLY MAILLET	1-7-16	—	After an hour and a half intense bombardment the Infantry commenced the assault, and the Brigade proceeded to positions of *readiness* in a hollow between MAILLY MAILLET and AUCHONVILLERS. Infantry reached, without difficulty, the first three enemy lines along the Corps front, but not having consolidated the trenches they had taken, were unable to retain their objective and, except in a few places, retired back on to the original line. The 36th Division were attacking on our right and the 4th Division on our left. The Brigade under orders from 29th Division returned to the position behind MAILLY MAILLET. Orders were received for "A" and "C" Batteries to be attached to 31st Division and they went into action south of COLIN CAMPS the same evening. 29th Division lost heavily in the assault on BEAUMONT HAMEL, but the losses were equalized by the success on the remainder of the front.	1.R
MAILLY MAILLET	2-7-16	—	Bombardment continued all along the front without any	

WAR DIARY

or

INTELLIGENCE SUMMARY.

(Erase heading not required.)

Army Form C. 2118.

Instructions regarding War Diaries and Intelligence Summaries are contained in F. S. Regs., Part II. and the Staff Manual respectively. Title pages will be prepared in manuscript.

Place	Date	Hour	Summary of Events and Information	Remarks and references to Appendices
	2/7/16 Cont'd		very definite results. Brigade Headquarters remained behind	1st R.
			MAILLY MAILLET, Battery Wagon Lines returned to ST. LEGER.	
ST. LEGER	3-7-16		Brigade Headquarters returned to ST. LEGER.	1st R.
ST. LEGER	4-7-16		"A" and "B" Batteries came out of action and returned to	
			ST. LEGER and COUIN respectively.	1st R
ST. LEGER	5-7-16		Orders received for the Brigade to relieve 31st Division, in	
			positions just north of COLINCAMPS - Lucrecie Avenue.	
			Relief took place during the day.	1st R
COLINCAMPS	6-7-16		Brigade Front extends from north of John Copse in	
			K.23.d. to K.29. B.1.0, including SERRE. Firing day and	
			night was kept up continually with an allowance of	
			120 rounds her gun her day. Orders were received to	
			keep wire cut, and to harass the enemy in every	
			possible manner.	1st R.
COLINCAMPS	7-7-16		Various small bombardments carried out. Report	
			received CONTALMAISON taken by the British, and	

Army Form C. 2118.

WAR DIARY
or
INTELLIGENCE SUMMARY.
(Erase heading not required.)

Instructions regarding War Diaries and Intelligence Summaries are contained in F. S. Regs., Part II. and the Staff Manual respectively. Title pages will be prepared in manuscript.

Place	Date	Hour	Summary of Events and Information	Remarks and references to Appendices
	7-7-16 Cont.d		everything in the south progressing favourably.	I.R.C.
COLINCAMPS	8-7-16		Nothing to report.	I.R.C.
COLINCAMPS	9-7-16		Nothing to report. Enemy inactive.	I.R.C.
COURCELLES	10-7-16		Brigade Headquarters moved to COURCELLES-AU-BOIS. Small bombardments carried out each night.	I.R.C. I.R.C.
COURCELLES	11-7-16		Nothing to report.	
COURCELLES	12-7-16		Continual activity kept up on enemy communication trenches and gaps in the wire. British progress reported in the south. Occasional raids attempted along the Army Front.	I.R.C.
COURCELLES	13-7-16		British reported at CONTALMAISON. Enemy artillery activity opposite this sector very slight. Guns appear to be firing from greater range.	I.R.C.
COURCELLES	14-7-16		Nothing to report.	I.R.C.
COURCELLES	15-7-16		Nothing to report.	I.R.C.
COURCELLES	16-7-16		British progress continued in the south. OVILLERS fell into our hands during the night and our troops were	

WAR DIARY
or
INTELLIGENCE SUMMARY.
(Erase heading not required.)

Army Form C. 2118.

Place	Date	Hour	Summary of Events and Information	Remarks and references to Appendices
	16-7-16 Cont'd		reported to hold the outskirts of POZIÈRES.	
COURCELLES	17-7-16	-	Nothing to report.	
COURCELLES	18-7-16	-	Nothing to report. Operations suspended owing to bad weather.	
COURCELLES	19-7-16	-	Nothing to report.	
COURCELLES	20-7-16	-	Brigade came out of action. Relieved by 38th Division, and returned to Wagon Lines at ST. LEGER.	
ST. LEGER	21-7-16	-	Brigade left ST. LEGER at 6.30a.m. and marched via BOUZINCOURT to AVELUY, where the Brigade took over from 12th Divisional Artillery. "B" Battery was split up, to make, with "A" and "C" Batteries, two 6 gun Batteries. In addition, D/240 Howitzers and C/240 and half B/240 were attached to the Brigade to form the Left Group, 48th Division, commanded by Lt. Col. F.C.B. WEST. Our infantry were holding the line running east of CONTALMAISON through the south of POZIÈRES in a line towards AUTHUILLE.	
AVELUY	22-7-16	-	Preparatory bombardment opened at 8.30p.m. and in the early	

Army Form C. 2118.

WAR DIARY
or
INTELLIGENCE SUMMARY.
(Erase heading not required.)

Place	Date	Hour	Summary of Events and Information	Remarks and references to Appendices
AVELUY	23-7-16		morning of the 23rd an attack was made on POZIÈRES by the Australian Division, and on the trenches west of it, X.2.a and b, by the 48th Division. Violent resistance was met with in both sectors but the Australians succeeded in getting through the southern half of POZIÈRES, during the day. 48th Division pressed forward on the left but were unable to consolidate except with their right flank which advanced a few hundred yards.	I.L
AVELUY	24-7-16.		The Australians reported through POZIÈRES, with the exception of the Cemetery. 143rd Brigade of the 48th Division was engaged in consolidating POZIÈRE line. The left flank of the 48th Division still unable to gain ground. Casualties:- Killed in action, Capt. A.E. STONE, "A" Battery, two other ranks wounded.	I.L
AVELUY	25-7-16		Nothing to report.	I.L
AVELUY	26-7-16		Nothing to report.	I.L

Army Form C. 2118.

WAR DIARY
or
INTELLIGENCE SUMMARY.
(Erase heading not required.)

Instructions regarding War Diaries and Intelligence Summaries are contained in F. S. Regs., Part II. and the Staff Manual respectively. Title pages will be prepared in manuscript.

Place	Date	Hour	Summary of Events and Information	Remarks and references to Appendices
AVELUY	27.7.16	—	Nothing to report.	
BOUZINCOURT	28.7.16	—	Divisional Artillery relieved in action by 12th Divl. Arty. Brigade returned to its Wagon Lines behind BOUZINCOURT for the night.	[ref]
AMPLIERS	29.7.16	—	Brigade marched to AMPLIERS via HEDAUVILLE and LOUVENCOURT.	[ref]
ST. OUEN	30.7.16	—	Brigade marched to ST. OUEN via DOULLENS, FIENVILLERS and DOMART and encamped by the side of the river on the west side of the village.	[ref]
ST. OUEN	31.7.16	—	Nothing to report.	

48th Divisional Artillery.

243rd (South Midland) BRIGADE

ROYAL FIELD ARTILLERY

AUGUST 1 9 1 6

Vol 1.8

CONFIDENTIAL.

WAR DIARY

of

243rd Brigade, R. F. A.

From 1st August, 1916 To 31st August, 1916.

(Volume 25).

[signature] Lt. & Adjt.
243 S. Mid. Field Arty. Bge.

Army Form C. 2118.

WAR DIARY
or
INTELLIGENCE SUMMARY.
(Erase heading not required.)

Instructions regarding War Diaries and Intelligence Summaries are contained in F. S. Regs., Part II. and the Staff Manual respectively. Title pages will be prepared in manuscript.

Place	Date	Hour	Summary of Events and Information	Remarks and references to Appendices
ST. OUEN	1-8-16	—	Nothing to report.	
ST. OUEN	2-8-16	—	Nothing to report.	
ST. OUEN	3-8-16	—	Drill Order in the morning.	
ST. OUEN	4-8-16	—	Gunners instructed in rifle exercises.	
ST. OUEN	5-8-16	—	Officers driving. Battery Staffs' parade.	
ST. OUEN	6-8-16	—	Nothing to report.	
ST. OUEN	7-8-16	—	Officers driving. Battery Staffs' parade.	
ST. OUEN	8-8-16	—	Drill Order.	
AMPLIER	9-8-16	—	Brigade marched via FIENVILLERS - CANDAS - BEAUVAL to AMPLIER and encamped in the same lines as were previously occupied.	
AMPLIER	10-8-16	—	Nothing to report.	
AMPLIER	11-8-16	—	Nothing to report.	
BOUZINCOURT	12-8-16	—	The Brigade marched back to the former wagon lines behind BOUZINCOURT, by the same route as before.	
OVILLERS	13-8-16	—	Personnel of 48th Divisional Artillery relieved 12th Divisional Artillery in action. The three Batteries of this Brigade took	

WAR DIARY
or
INTELLIGENCE SUMMARY.
(Erase heading not required.)

Army Form C. 2118.

Place	Date	Hour	Summary of Events and Information	Remarks and references to Appendices
	13-8-16 Cont'd		over positions in "MASH VALLEY" just south of OVILLERS-la-BOISSELLE, and together with C/240 and half B/240 and D/240 formed the LEFT GROUP of the 48th Division, under the command of Lt. Col. F.C.B. WEST.	J.L.
OVILLERS	14-8-16		During the night the enemy counter attacked and captured the trench lately taken by the 12th Division in R.33.a.8.1. to X.2.b.7.8. (sheet 57D 1/20000).	J.L.
OVILLERS	15-8-16		This trench was re-taken by the Right Brigade of 48th Division, but an attack made by the Australian Division on MOUQUET FARM was unsuccessful. The Left Brigade 48th Division in X.2.c and b. were unable to gain any ground either on the night 14th/15th, when attempted by 6th Battalion GLOUCESTER REGT, or on the night 15th/16th, when attempted by 4th Battalion, GLOUCESTER REGT. All attacks above ground were held up by machine gun fire, and bombing parties proceeding down the trenches were blocked by wire entanglements.	J.L.

Army Form C. 2118.

WAR DIARY
or
INTELLIGENCE SUMMARY.
(Erase heading not required.)

Instructions regarding War Diaries and Intelligence Summaries are contained in F. S. Regs., Part II. and the Staff Manual respectively. Title pages will be prepared in manuscript.

Place	Date	Hour	Summary of Events and Information	Remarks and references to Appendices
OVILLERS	16-8-16	—	Nothing to report.	I.R.
OVILLERS	17-8-16	—	144th Brigade relieved by the 143rd Brigade in the OVILLERS Sector.	I.R.
OVILLERS	18-8-16	5 p.m.	We opened a barrage on enemy's front line X.2.a & c., lifting after five minutes to the enemy's second line. Our Infantry crept up under the barrage and assaulted the enemy's line the moment the barrage lifted. The enemy were taken completely by surprise and our line was advanced up to X.2.a.25 – 4.b – 5.b – 9.b. (Sheet 57.D 20,000) About 500 prisoners were passed back during the evening and night. "B" Battery split up to make "A and C" into two gun Batteries.	I.R.
OVILLERS	19-8-16		Bombing was continued up the trenches and the line consolidated. points were established, and the line consolidated.	I.R.
OVILLERS	20-8-16		The two guns belonging to "C"/240 Battery attached, were lent to 25th Division to replace casualties to equipment. By bombing up trenches the Infantry proceeded up so far	

T2134. Wt. W708—776. 500000. 4/15. Sir J. C. & S.

WAR DIARY
or
INTELLIGENCE SUMMARY.

(Erase heading not required.)

Army Form C. 2118.

Place	Date	Hour	Summary of Events and Information	Remarks and references to Appendices
	20-8-16 Cont'd		at X.2.a.1.9 & 7.9. A strong footing was established in the LEIPZIG SALIENT in X.1.a.7.9.	1.16
OVILLERS	21-8-16		In the evening the 144th Brigade carried out an attack on the following objectives:- R.31.d.8.1. to R.32.c.1.5. and the German front and second lines between X.1.& 8.1 and R.31.d.7.3, X.1.a.9.8, R.31.c.9.5. Attack was successful and enemy's support line on a frontage of about 900 yards to a depth of 400 yards was occupied. About 210 prisoners were captured and our losses were very slight, since the infantry followed so close on the artillery barrage that the German garrisons were surprised in their dug-outs.	1.16
OVILLERS	22-8-16		Enemy carried out a surprise attack dressed in khaki on Points X.2.a.2.9 and 1.9. Both these points were subsequently recaptured.	1.16
OVILLERS	23-8-16		Enemy made another attack on Point X.2.a.1.9 at 1 am.	

WAR DIARY
or
INTELLIGENCE SUMMARY.
(Erase heading not required.)

Army Form C. 2118.

Place	Date	Hour	Summary of Events and Information	Remarks and references to Appendices
	23-8-16	Cont.d	and were driven off with considerable losses. 2nd Worcesters and 1st Wilts on our left attacked the Hindenburg trench – R.31.d.6.8. to R.31.c.7.6.6.+6. The objective was gained without serious opposition except on the left. Total number of prisoners taken amounted to 2 Officers and 140 Other Ranks.	
OVILLERS	24-8-16		A relief appeared to be taking place in the enemy trenches. Dummy bombardments were carried out during the day.	I.R.
OVILLERS	25-8-16			I.R.
OVILLERS	26-8-16		Nothing to report.	I.R.
OVILLERS	27-8-16		At 7pm. after a short bombardment, 143 and 145 Brigades attacked the line R.32.c.1.5.-33-9.1. These objectives were reached with very little loss.	I.R.
BOUZINCOURT	28-8-16		Group was relieved by the 25th Division. Brigade Hed. Qrs. returned to Wagon Lines at BOUZINCOURT and "A" and "C" Batteries each with a section of "B" attached, went into action north of MESNIL, where they were grouped together	

WAR DIARY
or
INTELLIGENCE SUMMARY.

(Erase heading not required.)

Army Form C. 2118.

Place	Date	Hour	Summary of Events and Information	Remarks and references to Appendices
	28-8-16 Cont.d		with #9th Divisional Artillery to engage the trenches between THIEPVAL and the River ANCRE.	
BOUZINCOURT	29.8.16		Nothing to report.	
BOUZINCOURT	30.8.16		Nothing to report.	
BOUZINCOURT	31.8.16		Nothing to report.	

48th. DIVISIONAL ARTILLERY

243rd. BRIGADE   R. F. A.

SEPTEMBER 1916.

<u>Confidential.</u>

War Diary
of
243rd (S.M.) Bde. R.F.A.

From 1st September, 1916 To 30th September, 1916.

(Volume 36).

Lt. and Adjt.
243rd Brigade, R.F.A.

Army Form C. 2118.

WAR DIARY
or
INTELLIGENCE SUMMARY.
(Erase heading not required.)

Instructions regarding War Diaries and Intelligence Summaries are contained in F. S. Regs., Part II. and the Staff Manual respectively. Title pages will be prepared in manuscript.

Place	Date	Hour	Summary of Events and Information	Remarks and references to Appendices
BOUZINCOURT	1.9.16	—	Nothing to report.	
BOUZINCOURT	2.9.16	—	Nothing to report.	
BOUZINCOURT	3.9.16	—	Nothing to report.	
BOUZINCOURT	4.9.16	—	Nothing to report.	
BOUZINCOURT	5.9.16	—	Nothing to report.	
BOUZINCOURT	6.9.16	—	Nothing to report.	
BOUZINCOURT	7.9.16	—	The Batteries left their position, with the exception of a small guard on the guns, and returned to the Wagon Lines.	
BOUZINCOURT	8.9.16	—	Nothing to report.	
BOUZINCOURT	9.9.16	—	One gun per Battery sent to the I.O.M. as all the guns were urgently in need of overhaul.	
BOUZINCOURT	10.9.16	—	Nothing to report.	
BOUZINCOURT	11.9.16	—	Nothing to report.	
BOUZINCOURT	12.9.16	—	Nothing to report.	
BOUZINCOURT	13.9.16	—	2nd and 3rd Brigades were put into positions North and West of MESNIL to assist in the capture of the Wonder Work and a trench	

Army Form C. 2118.

WAR DIARY
or
INTELLIGENCE SUMMARY.
(Erase heading not required.)

Place	Date	Hour	Summary of Events and Information	Remarks and references to Appendices
	13-9-16 Cont.d		parallel to the HOHENZOLLERN to the south of THIEPVAL, occupied by the 11th Division.	J.M.L.
BOUZINCOURT	14-9-16	-	This was successfully carried out at 6.30pm and the Brigade returned to the Wagon Lines early the following morning with Orders were	J.M.L.
BOUZINCOURT	15-9-16	-	orders to be ready to move at two hours notice. Orders were received to move at 3pm. and the 240 and 243 Brigades, starting at 3pm, marched via BOUZINCOURT and ALBERT to a position east of OVILLERS in order to give support to the Canadians for the attack on the line between COURCELETTE and MOUQUET FARM.	J.M.L.
OVILLERS	16-9-16	-	Canadians successfully took COURCELETTE and part of the ZOLLERN GRABEN.	J.M.L.
OVILLERS	17-9-16	-	The Canadians reported holding MOUQUET FARM and the line running east along the railway line to COURCELETTE, including the southern end of the ZOLLERN GRABEN.	J.M.L.
OVILLERS	18-9-16	-	Nothing to report.	

Army Form C. 2118.

WAR DIARY
or
INTELLIGENCE SUMMARY.
(Erase heading not required.)

Instructions regarding War Diaries and Intelligence Summaries are contained in F. S. Regs., Part II. and the Staff Manual respectively. Title pages will be prepared in manuscript.

Place	Date	Hour	Summary of Events and Information	Remarks and references to Appendices
OVILLERS	19.9.16	—	A few shell fell round the Hd. Qrs. of the 240 and 243 Brigades just east of OVILLERS, and destroyed the officers mess of the former, killing two officers and wounding two officers and one other rank, including Capt. H.H.d'E. VALLANCEY of 4/243 Bty.	
OVILLERS	20.9.16	—	Brigade Hd. Qrs. moved back to USNA REDOUBT.	
OVILLERS	21.9.16	—	Nothing to report.	
OVILLERS	22.9.16	—	Nothing to report.	
OVILLERS	23.9.16	—	Canadians reported holding HIGH TRENCH, running north of MOUQUET FARM, having entered it they found it unoccupied.	
OVILLERS	24.9.16	—	Nothing to report.	
OVILLERS	25.9.16	—	Enemy recaptured HIGH TRENCH and MOUQUET FARM.	
OVILLERS	26.9.16	—	An attack was carried out at 12.35 p.m. on the line running east from THIEPVAL to the north of COURCELETTE. The first two objectives were successfully reached, and a line established running from the north of THIEPVAL, along ZOLLERN TRENCH, to R 22.c.3.8. About 800 prisoners were captured including 25 officers.	

WAR DIARY
or
INTELLIGENCE SUMMARY.
(Erase heading not required.)

Army Form C. 2118.

Place	Date	Hour	Summary of Events and Information	Remarks and references to Appendices
OVILLERS	27.9.16	—	Further progress was made on our left and the STUFF REDOUBT in R.21.c. was captured.	J.L.
OVILLERS	28.9.16	—	At 1 p.m. an attack was made on the SCHWABEN REDOUBT, just north of THIEPVAL, and the larger part of it was captured. At 6 p.m. an unsuccessful attempt was made on our front to take HESSIAN TRENCH in R.21.d. Casualties – Lt.Col. F.C.B.WEST killed by shell-fire; Other Ranks wounded 2. Lt.Col. J.R.COLVILLE, D.S.O., 241st (S.M.) Brigade took over temporary Command of the RIGHT GROUP. Forward positions were reconnoitred for three batteries south of MOUQUET FARM, and "C"/240 moved up their Battery into position just North of POZIÈRES. Major CONSTANTINE, C/243 Bty, took Command of the Brigade.	J.L.
OVILLERS	29.9.16	—	An attack was made at 12 noon on the HESSIAN TRENCH, which was successfully taken. Part of it, however, was lost later in the evening as a result of enemy counter attacks on the north east. The northern side of the SCHWABEN REDOUBT	J.L.

Place	Date	Hour	Summary of Events and Information	Remarks and references to Appendices
	29.9.16 Cont.d	-	was also retaken by the enemy. Orders were received that the 48th Divisional Artillery would be relieved by the 25th Divisional Artillery in action. One section per Battery was relieved by them the same night. Attempts were made during the night to capture by bombing attacks, a portion of the trenches which had been lost. These were not, however, entirely successful, and the situation in the morning was nearly the same.	1st L
OVILLERS	30.9.16		Operations were carried out on our left to re-capture the STUFF REDOUBT. All objectives were gained.	1st L Map used:- Sheet 57D SE 1/20,000

CONFIDENTIAL

WAR DIARY.

of

243rd (S.M.) Brigade, R. F. A.

From 1st October   to   18th October, 1916.

(Volume 27)

Lt. and Adjt.
243rd Brigade, R.F.A.

Army Form C. 2118.

WAR DIARY
or
INTELLIGENCE SUMMARY.
(Erase heading not required.)

Instructions regarding War Diaries and Intelligence Summaries are contained in F.S. Regs., Part II. and the Staff Manual respectively. Title pages will be prepared in manuscript.

Place	Date	Hour	Summary of Events and Information	Remarks and references to Appendices
OVILLERS	1-10-16	—	48th Divisional Artillery relieved in action by the 25th Divisional Artillery, and returned to Wagon Lines.	J.L.
WARLINCOURT	2-10-16	—	The Brigade marched via BOUZINCOURT, LOUVENCOURT and AUTHIE to Wagon Lines at WARLINCOURT.	J.L.
WARLINCOURT	3-10-16	—	Orders received for the Divisional Artillery to split up into two 18-pdr. and one Howitzer Group, to cover the line along the southern edge of GOMMECOURT PARK. Group Commanders reconnoitred O.Ps. and Battery Positions.	J.L.
WARLINCOURT	4-10-16	—	A and B batteries with one section of C each formed two 6-gun batteries at K.14.d.4.8 and K.7.a.1.7. respectively.	J.L.
WARLINCOURT	5-10-16	—	B Battery occupied their position during the night 5/6th.	J.L.
WARLINCOURT	6-10-16	—	The working party at A Battery position were shelled out and compelled to abandon the spot and the guns were unable to proceed into action that night.	J.L.
WARLINCOURT	7-10-16	—	A new position was chosen for A battery, in K.14.C.	J.L.

Army Form C. 2118.

WAR DIARY
or
INTELLIGENCE SUMMARY.
(Erase heading not required.)

Instructions regarding War Diaries and Intelligence Summaries are contained in F. S. Regs., Part II. and the Staff Manual respectively. Title pages will be prepared in manuscript.

Place	Date	Hour	Summary of Events and Information	Remarks and references to Appendices
WARLINCOURT	8.10.16	—	"A" Battery moved into their new position.	A.P.K.
WARLINCOURT	9.10.16	—	Registration carried out daily. Enemy activity normal.	A.P.K.
WARLINCOURT	10.10.16	—	Nothing to report.	A.P.K.
WARLINCOURT	11.10.16	—	Nothing to report.	A.P.K.
WARLINCOURT	12.10.16	—	Nothing to report.	A.P.K.
WARLINCOURT	13.10.16	—	Orders were received for the reorganization of Brigades, to form two Brigades of three 6-gun 18-pr Batteries and one 4-gun 4.5" How'r Battery; and one Brigade of two 6-gun 18-prs Batteries and one 4-gun 4.5" How'r Battery.	A.P.K.
WARLINCOURT	14.10.16	—	Nothing to report.	A.P.K.
WARLINCOURT	15.10.16	—	Nothing to report.	A.P.K.
WARLINCOURT	16.10.16	—	Owing to three Divisions being withdrawn the Divisional Artillery had to extend to cover a larger front.	A.P.K.
WARLINCOURT	17.10.16	—	Nothing to report.	A.P.K.
WARLINCOURT	18.10.16	—	The reorganization of Brigades took place. A/243 Battery and half C/243 Battery were posted to 240 Brigade. B/243 Battery	

Army Form C. 2118.

WAR DIARY
or
INTELLIGENCE SUMMARY.
(Erase heading not required.)

Instructions regarding War Diaries and Intelligence Summaries are contained in F. S. Regs., Part II. and the Staff Manual respectively. Title pages will be prepared in manuscript.

Place	Date	Hour	Summary of Events and Information	Remarks and references to Appendices
	18-10-16	cont.	and half C/243 Battery were posted to 241 Brigade. 243 Brigade ceased to exist. Headquarters 243 Brigade was divided up between Hd. Qrs. 240 Brigade, D/240 Battery and D/241 Battery	

The writer(s) has/~~have~~ NOT been informed of the
action taken by this office.

13491. COMERFORD. E.G. 1914-18
Collation

(signature)
Colonel;
Officer-in-Charge,
Royal Artillery Records.

CC

Mr Sullivan

Can you assist, please

A Bruce

Seat "A"

www.ingramcontent.com/pod-product-compliance
Lightning Source LLC
Chambersburg PA
CBHW081540160426
43191CB00011B/1803